Runaway Train

Youth with Emotional Disturbance

YOUTH WITH SPECIAL NEEDS

Runaway Train

Youth with Emotional Disturbance

BY AUTUMN LIBAL

MASON CREST PUBLISHERS

Mason Crest Publishers Inc.
370 Reed Road
Broomall, Pennsylvania 19008
(866) MCP-BOOK (toll free)

First printing
1 2 3 4 5 6 7 8 9 10
Libal, Autumn.
Runaway train: youth with emotional disturbance / by Autumn Libal.
p. cm.‾(Youth with special needs)
Summary: Tells the story of Sheila, a high school student suffering from severe emotional disturbance, and her attempts to cope by venting her rage, cutting herself, and starving herself before getting the help she needs to begin to recover. Includes bibliographical references and index.
1. Behavior disorders in children‾Juvenile literature. 2. Problem youth‾Juvenile literature. 3. Mentally ill children‾Juvenile literature. 4. Problem children‾Juvenile literature. 5. Adolescent psychotherapy‾Juvenile literature. [1. Emotional problems.] I. Title. II. Series.
RJ506.B44L53 2004
618.92'89‾dc22   2003018437

ISBN 1-59084-732-6
1-59084-727-X (series)

Design by Harding House Publishing Service.
Composition by Bytheway Publishing Services, Inc., Binghamton, New York.
Cover art by Keith Rosko.
Cover design by Benjamin Stewart.
Produced by Harding House Publishing Service, Vestal, New York.
Printed and bound in the Hashemite Kingdom of Jordan.

Contents

A child with special needs is not defined by his disability.
It is just one part of who he is.

INTRODUCTION

Each child is unique and wonderful. And some children have differences we call special needs. Special needs can mean many things. Sometimes children will learn differently, or hear with an aid, or read with Braille. A young person may have a hard time communicating or paying attention. A child can be born with a special need, or acquire it by an accident or through a health condition. Sometimes a child will be developing in a typical manner and then become delayed in that development. But whatever problems a child may have with her learning, emotions, behavior, or physical body, she is always a person first. She is not defined by her disability; instead, the disability is just one part of who she is.

Inclusion means that young people with and without special needs are together in the same settings. They learn together in school; they play together in their communities; they all have the same opportunities to belong. Children learn so much from each other. A child with a hearing impairment, for example, can teach another child a new way to communicate using sign language. Someone else who has a physical disability affecting his legs can show his friends how to play wheelchair basketball. Children with and without special needs can teach each other how to appreciate and celebrate their differences. They can also help each other discover how people are more alike than they are different. Understanding and appreciating how we all have similar needs helps us learn empathy and sensitivity.

In this series, you will read about young people with special needs from the unique perspectives of children and adolescents who are experiencing the disability firsthand. Of course, not all children with a particular disability are the same as the characters in the stories. But the stories demonstrate at an emotional level how a special need impacts a child, his family, and his friends. The factual material in each chapter will expand your horizons by adding to your knowledge about a particular disability. The series as a whole will help you understand differences better and appreciate how they make us all stronger and better.

—*Cindy Croft*
Educational Consultant

YOUTH WITH SPECIAL NEEDS provides a unique forum for demystifying a wide variety of childhood medical and developmental disabilities. Written to captivate an adolescent audience, the books bring to life the challenges and triumphs experienced by children with common chronic conditions such as hearing loss, mental retardation, physical differences, and speech difficulties. The topics are addressed frankly through a blend of fiction and fact. Students and teachers alike can move beyond the information provided by accessing the resources offered at the end of each text.

This series is particularly important today as the number of children with special needs is on the rise. Over the last two decades, advances in pediatric medical techniques have allowed children who have chronic illnesses and disabilities to live longer, more functional lives. As a result, these children represent an increasingly visible part of North American population in all aspects of daily life. Students are exposed to peers with special needs in their classrooms, through extracurricular activities, and in the community. Often, young people have misperceptions and unanswered questions about a child's disabilities—and more important, his or her *abilities*. Many times, there is no vehicle for talking about these complex issues in a comfortable manner.

This series provides basic information that will leave readers with a deeper understanding of each condition, along with an awareness of some of the associated emotional impacts on affected children, their families, and their peers. It will also encourage further conversation about these issues. Most important, the series promotes a greater comfort for its readers as they live, play, and work side by side with these individuals who have medical and developmental differences—youth with special needs.

—Dr. Lisa Albers, Dr. Carolyn Bridgemohan, Dr. Laurie Glader
Medical Consultants

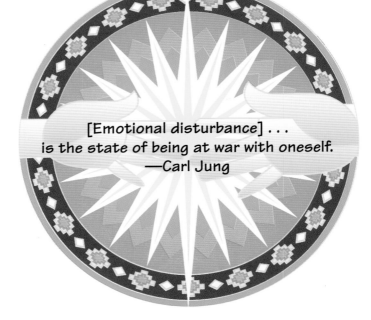

[Emotional disturbance] . . .
is the state of being at war with oneself.
—Carl Jung

1

SHEILA'S RAGE

Sheila's pen burned across the paper, leaving scrawling black lines in its wake. These were lonely hours—the times when she came home from school too angry for tears. This was most of the time, really. Sheila would walk the entire way home with her head down, barely looking for traffic as she crossed the busy streets, her body rigid, and her posture daring the world to speak a word to her—the word that might make her snap. When she reached her apartment building, she would throw open the door, reveling in the violent bang it made as the old hinges gave a twisted scream. Then she'd race up the two flights, combat boots pounding out her anger on the creaking stairs. Once in her apartment, if her younger sister Megan was already home, Sheila would pick a fight. If not, she'd go straight to her room and write her rage into a book of secrets and dark poetry.

I'd rather die than set foot in that school one more time, she wrote today. *Those girls in my class are all liars. I'd like to feed them dirt and then watch them gag on it.* She rubbed the back of her hand across her eye, smudging dark makeup down her cheek. *Today Leslie Johnson yelled down the hall, "Hey, Sheila! You're a freak!" I didn't know what to say, but everyone started snickering, so I turned around and yelled back, 'You wanna come say that to my face?' Everybody shut up for a minute. But when I got out of class, I saw that someone had scrawled, "Die Freak" right across the front of my locker . . . in red lipstick. I rubbed and rubbed at it with my shirtsleeve, but now there's just a big smudge running like blood down the front of my locker door.*

Frustrated and not knowing what else to say, Sheila chewed her pen while her anger mounted. *I'd like to see that whole building go up in flames with everyone locked inside.* She wrote the final word with an aggressive flourish, then threw the book across the room. The book smacked the wall like a giant bug against a windshield. It seemed to hang suspended for a moment, pages flapping like hundreds of desperately beating wings. Then it collapsed lifelessly to the ground. Sheila stood, retrieved the book, and opened to the page where she had been writing. This time she wrote in a long, uninterrupted stream, her fingers aching as her pen bit into the paper.

When you spit those words
That drilled in my head
I squeezed my fist
Until it bled
Then I slit my throat
Now I'm almost dead
Tryin' to forget
All those things you said

You think you know me
But you're really blind
Don't see me coming
And I don't mind
Cause I'll crush you
Beat you
Burn you out
Chew you up and swallow
Till there is no doubt
That your thoughtless words
Are gonna make you sore
Cause I'm not gonna take
Your lies anymore.

When Sheila finished writing her lines of poetry, she closed the book and laid back, exhausted on her bed. A sculpture of twisted metal and mutilated Barbie™ dolls hung from the ceiling above her. It had been Sheila's freshman art project. She had surgically removed each of the doll's breasts with a steak knife, then impaled the severed organs on sharp wires. Next, she had stuck pins into the dolls' too-blue eyes, made nooses from their blond hair, wrapped the silky ropes about their necks, and hung them with their beauty. She called it, *What I Think of Femininity*. Sheila felt that most of her classmates were too stupid to understand her piece of art; they were all such **conformists** that they could never accept anything different from themselves. Sheila nursed her bitterness as the sculpture turned like some crazy mobile in a young girl's nightmare.

Hours later when her father finally returned home from work, Sheila was still lying on her bed staring straight up at the ceiling. A tentative knock rapped on the other side of her bedroom door.

"Sheila, are you in there?" Her father's voice sounded tired and apprehensive. Sheila did not answer. "Have you eaten?" he tried again. The hours of quiet had brought on a feeling of numbness and calm, but now Sheila could sense the anger rising again. She struggled against it.

"Go away," she mumbled, speaking quietly in an attempt to keep control.

"Megan made dinner," her father continued. Sheila could tell by the sound of his voice that he was running his hand through his hair and shuffling his feet. For some reason, this made her even angrier. Why did he even bother? Why couldn't he just leave her alone?

"I'm not hungry," Sheila replied, her voice rising and her breath quickening. She felt her rage coming, and soon it would be too late to stop. She wished her father would just give up. Was he stupid? Didn't he know that he was only making things worse? Sheila sucked air through her teeth and hoped her father would leave before she exploded. But he spoke again.

"Come on, Sheila. It's good. Your sister worked very hard to make a nice dinner for us and . . ."

It was too much. Her father's attempt at encouragement sent Sheila over the edge. She shot up in bed and screamed at the closed door. "And I hope you both choke on it!" She leapt to her feet and tore her sheets from her bed. "Why can't anyone ever leave me alone?" Her lamp crashed to the ground, shards of brown pottery smashing in every direction. Sheila kicked the broken pieces, sending them spinning, then grabbed the nightstand and heaved it onto the remains of the lamp. "Is everybody stupid?" Her screams continued as she grabbed three jars of paint from her dresser. "I HATE YOU!" The jars of paint exploded against the door like punctuation marks for her words. In the hall outside the room, there was silence. Black, red, and blue paint oozed down the wood, a grand finale to Sheila's performance. Panting, Sheila stared at the broken glass and pottery littering her bedroom floor. As the tears finally bubbled up, she felt a strange sense of awe descending upon her.

"What is wrong with me?" she whispered as she sank down on her bed and cried.

Late that night, when her father and sister were safely in bed, Sheila ventured from her room, nausea and hunger warring in her stomach. Standing in the greenish-white light of the refrigerator, she searched for remains of Megan's dinner until the smell of rotting vegetables forced her to close the door. On the counter, a carefully wrapped plate of food sat with a note on top. Sheila picked up the note and held it to the microwave's clock. By the electric-orange glow, she could just make out the words, *I saved this for you.—Meg.* Hunger winning the war inside her, Sheila peeled back the cellophane from the plate and took a tentative bite. Her father was right; it was good. Sheila ate reluctantly while guilt invaded her heart.

Sheila allowed her rage, so potent and uncontrollable just hours ago, to recede to the back of her emotions. At night, when everything was dark and silent, it was safe to release, to risk letting other emotions through. As the tide of her anger went out, regret welled in the hollows left behind. Minutes drifted by as Sheila stood in the empty kitchen, drowning in her private whirlpool of emotions. For Sheila, anger was heat, energy, power, and protection. It was a driving force that could not be controlled or denied. Sorrow, on the other hand, was dark and heavy. It dripped slow poison into her blood and suffocated her with its weight. Needing relief, Sheila pressed through the quicksand of emotion toward her father's bedroom door.

The door stood ajar, but Sheila could not see into the room. She leaned against the door frame. "Dad?" She sent the word as a scout into the darkness to judge whether her father was awake. Shadows slipped across the walls, and Sheila held her breath waiting for a response. The scout, however, reported silence. Sheila tried a little louder, "I'm really sorry, Dad." He seemed to be asleep. Sheila hesitated in the doorway, but did not speak again.

Across the room, Sheila's father lay motionless, eyes open in the dark. He heard the regret in his daughter's words and felt her turmoil hovering outside the room. He wondered if he should move, give some sign that he was awake, that he had heard her apology. But indecisiveness became inaction, and he did nothing. He did not move as her presence vibrated in the doorway, and he did not call out as she turned to walk away.

WHAT IS EMOTIONAL DISTURBANCE?

Emotional disturbance is a general term given to any condition involving emotional distress that is severe enough to impair a person's ability to function normally. There is a wide **spectrum** of experience that may constitute emotional disturbance. On the one hand, individuals may experience relatively mild forms of depression, anxiety, or low **self-esteem**. In more serious forms of emotional disturbance, the individual may begin displaying antisocial behavior by withdrawing from other people or breaking normal rules of social conduct. As symptoms worsen, however, individuals with emotional disturbance often begin abusing substances like alcohol and drugs or engaging in risky, even criminal behavior. In the most severe cases of emotional disturbance, individuals can become **suicidal**, **homicidal**, or **psychotic**.

Young adolescents are vulnerable to emotional disturbances.

A young person with an emotional disturbance will have difficulty functioning in the classroom.

An Educational Definition
with Legal Consequences

The phrase "emotional disturbance" is generally seen as an educational term rather than a psychiatric one. It means that whatever the individual's specific psychiatric diagnosis, her emotional symptoms interfere with her ability to learn in a school setting.

Since the 1970s, state and federal courts and governments have been passing laws that protect the rights of people with disabilities. These laws say that all people should have an opportunity to participate equally in society and should not be discriminated against because of special needs. These laws also protect children with emotional disturbance. Emotional disturbance may not seem like a "disability" at first, but it is a condition that severely impacts a young person's ability to learn and function well in a school setting. In the past, a child with emotional disturbance or other special needs could have been kicked out of classrooms or denied the ability to attend school. Thanks to civil rights laws, however, individuals with conditions like emotional disturbance can no longer be discriminated against, and they have the ability to fight in court the people who do discriminate against them.

One specific example of the important laws protecting people with special needs is the Education for the Handicapped Act. This landmark act was passed in 1975 and was known as Public Law 94-142. Today a new version of this law exists as the Individuals with Disabilities Education Act (IDEA). This law requires (among other things) that state and federal governments give money to schools to meet the special educational, emotional, and physical needs of individuals with disabilities, ages three to twenty-one. Before these landmark laws, children with disabilities like emotional disturbance were not guaranteed the right to an appropriate education. Young people were commonly placed in hospitals or institutions for the mentally ill, continued on destructive paths until they broke laws and were imprisoned, or were simply shunned from the rest of society. Society was apt to view individuals with any disabilities with suspicion, condemning them (or their parents) for their problems. Thanks to laws like IDEA that insure equal treatment and proper education, many people have a better understanding of both the needs and of the abilities of people with conditions like emotional disturbance.

Variations in the Duration

A person may experience emotional disturbance for a short or for a long period of time. For example, many people will

Some very young children experience childhood schizophrenia, a serious emotional disturbance.

experience brief periods of emotional disturbance after traumatic events such as a terrible car accident or the death of a loved one. The person may have a temporary bout of depression, feel unable to interact with others, or be unable to perform her schoolwork or job duties. In most cases, however, the individual will feel better as time passes, and the emotional disturbance will resolve without further difficulties. The person may, of course, still feel sad when remembering the event, but she will not feel so emotionally disturbed that she is unable to function normally and continue with life.

On the other hand, people can suffer from **chronic** forms of emotional disturbance. For example, psychiatric disorders are one form of emotional disturbance. Someone suffering from a psychiatric disorder like **obsessive-compulsive disorder** or **schizophrenia** would have a more lasting form of emotional disturbance. As another example, a person who has experienced physical or emotional abuse from a young age will very likely develop some form of emotional disturbance as he grows and may have great difficulty recovering from this emotional disturbance even long after the abuse has ended. In cases like these, it is unlikely that the individual will be able to overcome his emotional disturbance on his own. The assistance of a trained mental-health professional will likely be required to help the person deal with his emotional disturbance. In such cases, different forms of **cognitive therapy** will likely be used to help the person examine and reinvent his emotional functioning, and psychiatric medications may, if appropriate, be used to treat psychiatric disorders. You can learn more about individual psychiatric disorders and how they are treated in the Mason Crest series PSYCHIATRIC DISORDERS: DRUGS AND PSYCHOLOGY FOR THE MIND AND BODY.

Chronic forms of emotional disturbance may become a part of the person's identity.

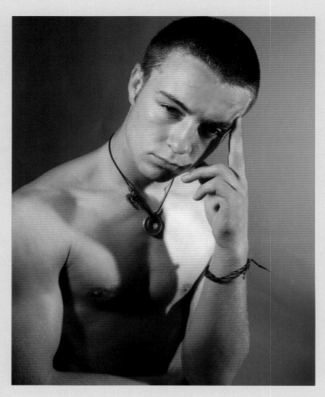

A person with an emotional disturbance may have difficulty concentrating. His emotions may seem overwhelming.

The Symptoms

There are many different types of emotional disturbance and many different symptoms or characteristics that a person with such a condition might display. To be diagnosed by a professional (such as a psychiatrist, social worker, or a school psychologist) as having emotional disturbance or to receive special assistance from one's school, a person must have at least one of the following symptoms, and the symptom must last for a long period of time:

- *Difficulty learning that is not caused by an intellectual or learning disability, by a sensory deficit, or by an existing health condition.* For example, a person having difficulty learning because of damage to the brain or a health problem that forces him to leave school often would not be diagnosed with an emotional disturbance. However, a child with no such medical history who is experiencing learning problems may be suffering from an emotional disturbance.
- *Difficulty developing or maintaining relationships with friends, teachers, and other people in the person's life.* Developing and maintaining healthy relationships with other people is an important part of having a well-adjusted, emotionally balanced life. An inability to build or sustain connections with other people is often the result of an emotional disturbance.
- *Behaving in a way that is unsuitable for normal circumstances or having feelings that are inappropriate, peculiar, or contrary to a situation.* For example, screaming at a teacher in a classroom, crying with sadness at a happy movie, or laughing during a discussion of someone's death would all be inappropriate or peculiar reactions. Screaming at someone and flying into a rage without significant **provocation** may be an isolated incident brought on by being bullied at school. Everyone has uncontrollable emotions sometimes, and succumbing to such a reaction does not mean one has emotional disturbance. However, if reactions like this are part of a typical pattern of behavior, they would be **indicative** of an emotional disturbance.
- *Having unhappiness or depression as one's prevailing mood over a long period of time.* Everyone experiences sadness, feelings of depression, and even extreme grief and despair at certain times in their lives.

A person's emotional disturbance can lead to physical symptoms of fatigue and pain.

However, if these emotions continue without change or improvement, they may be part of a more chronic form of emotional disturbance.

- *Developing acute anxiety and physical symptoms (such as **fatigue** or illness) because of personal, social, school, or work-related problems.* We all experience nervousness and **trepidation** sometimes, but when these feelings become severe enough to make a person feel physically ill and reoccur at the thought of interacting with others or going to school or work, the feelings may be indicative of an emotional disturbance.

All . . . symptoms have as their object the task of safeguarding the patient's self-esteem.
—Alfred Adler

2

TRENT'S SUBTERRANEAN WORLD

Sheila lay in bed waiting for the breakfast sounds to fade. At last she heard the front door close, once for her father, again for Megan. When she was sure she was alone, Sheila got out of bed. Debris from the night before lay scattered about her feet like skeletons. Sheila picked her way through the wreckage left by her tantrum. Last night her room had felt like a steaming jungle war zone. The paint had run like a living thing down the walls, and the glass and pottery had hummed with angry vibrations on the floor. In the morning light, the paint now dry and cracked and the broken shards lying silent, the room looked like a desert scattered with bones. Sheila felt like a mirage as she tiptoed over the barren landscape. She dressed in army-green pants and a slashed shirt, then looked into the mirror. A crack ran down the center of the glass, cutting a jagged scar into Sheila's reflection. Yesterday's makeup streaked down her face in trails of black tears. Sheila liked the affect, so she added a little more eyeliner to heighten the bruised and battered look.

In the kitchen, she called Trent. She knew he wouldn't be awake yet, but she let the phone ring until the answering machine picked up. "Don't go to school today," was the only message she left. She knew it was all he would need. Lately Sheila's grades had slipped from low B's and C's to D's and even F's, but she wasn't about to let that frighten her into going to school today. When she arrived at his dilapidated house, Trent would put last night's events into perspective. For Sheila,

27

the dawn had brought pain and remorse, emotions she detested, but Trent would give Sheila a whole new view of what had transpired. He would tell her the truth of her actions, fan her flames of anger, and banish all guilt to the far reaches of her unconscious.

Trent had sharp eyes, a brutal smile, and an inner rage that made Sheila's fits look like well-staged but harmless theatre. His voice was an oily mix of bitterness and cold rationality that always convinced Sheila she was justified in throwing firestorm fits. Now, in the sorrowful aftermath of one of these rages, Sheila needed Trent to soothe her pain the way an addict needs a drug. His words would penetrate her aching mind like a junkie's needle; he'd insert his magic serum of poisonous thoughts, and self-righteousness would spread through her soul.

Sheila could not remember how she and Trent became friends, but she remembered the first time she went to his house. It had been a sunny day, but the house's windows remained gray and impenetrable, as if the building cradled its own darkness inside. The front door had swung open at her touch, so she'd let herself in. Inside, the house smelled of mold, dust, and kitty litter. The only light flickered from a television in the living room. Trent's parents sat like wax figures, his father on the couch, his mother on a collapsing chair. Neither looked up when Sheila crept through the front door. She waited silently for a moment, afraid to speak lest the kitty-litter air invade her mouth, but finally she approached the living room. As she leaned forward to announce her presence, a hand grabbed her elbow from behind. Sheila spun around. It was Trent. Without a word, he led her from the room, down a narrow hall to a sagging door behind which was the stairway to the basement.

Sheila held her breath as she descended into Trent's subterranean world. As they walked, Trent pulled chains that dangled from the ceiling. Bare bulbs hummed to life. Down here, the air was damp, but had none of the fuzzy, ammonia-laden smells of the house above. Trent had cleaned the decaying cellar until it was almost sterile, but there was nothing sterile about the objects he'd created in this private place. On the wall across the room, a six-foot-tall dragon spread its wings over a metal-framed bed. Trent watched expressionless as Sheila walked in awe toward the wall, kneeled upon the squeaking mattress, and ran her hand over the paint, marveling at the lifelike details in the giant lizard's scales, the visible heat in the fire from its nostrils.

As Sheila explored the rest of the room, she noticed on another wall, in complete contrast to the carefully painted dragon, words were scrawled in ***manic*** letters, some in paint, pen, and pencil, others scratched directly into the gray surface. Some were single words—*flood, heartbeat, drum*. Others were phrases and snatches of poetry. One phrase read, *Beat me till your fists bleed, I'm drowning in your lunacy, but I will never scream.* Another said, *Everything is dark, so safely dark, but I can hear your footsteps in the hall.* Sheila shivered and turned her attention away from the wall.

The most impressive feature of Trent's basement home rose from the middle of the cement floor. It was a strange diorama, a meticulously created replica of the city. But upon closer inspection, Sheila realized that it wasn't really the city, but the city seen through warped eyes. Buildings bowed on crazy angles. Hills rose where in reality there were none. Vegetation blazed in unrealistic colors, and streets roamed without purpose—falling dead where they should not end, leading to alleys where people would never go, even lifting over buildings. Sheila stared in awe at the city. It made her own attempts at art look pathetically childish.

"How long have you been working on this?" she whispered. It was the first thing either one of them had said since she entered the house.

"Ten years. Since I was six," Trent replied.

"What are you going to do with it when it's done?" Sheila's admiration was obvious.

"Smash it," Trent replied matter-of-factly, not a hint of emotion tarnishing his voice. Sheila looked up. He was serious.

"How could you destroy something so incredible . . . something you created?" Trent did not even hesitate before giving a shrugged reply.

"God created **Sodom and Gomorra**, didn't he? Look what he did to them." Trent gave a crooked grin. Sheila had no idea what he was talking about, but she didn't want to appear stupid, so she grinned too. At school, all the teachers called Trent a troublemaker and an underachiever, but looking around the basement, Sheila felt sure he was a genius.

The morning after her latest fit of rage, Sheila waited two more hours before leaving for Trent's house. Upon arrival, she did not bother knocking at his door but simply pushed her way in. His parents sat like always in the living room. From day to day, their positions changed in front of the television, but Sheila had never actually seen them move. In the year she'd been coming to see Trent, his parents had become like zombies to her—frightening at first with their living-dead appearance, but so lifeless they were soon easy to ignore. The TV flickered soundlessly before them. Sheila passed the eerie fun-house scene unnoticed and descended into the basement.

The only light came from dusty streaks fighting around the edges of the basement's one boarded-up window. Sheila pulled the bare bulb's chain at the bottom of the stairs. Its soupy light revealed Trent sitting hunched over the diorama, peering intently at the building he had in one hand and brandishing a tiny paintbrush in the other.

"This better be good." He spoke without turning around. "I'm missing an appointment with Hambone for you." Trent's voice was listless and deadpan. Mr. Hammond was the high school counselor. He had a soft heart, but an even softer body. Due to his pudgy cheeks, squished nose, and short, fat body, students had been calling him Hambone for as long as anyone could remember. But Mr. Hammond pretended not to know and continued to do his best to help all the students in the school—even the most difficult and angry ones. Trent seized on Mr. Hammond's kind-heartedness and used it to eat him alive.

Had Sheila been speaking to anyone else, she would have been angered by the harsh tone, but she always wanted to please Trent and was knocked off balance by his unexpected remark. "But you hate seeing Hambone," she stammered, unable to understand why Trent would be upset at missing school.

"No, I love seeing Hambone." Trent slowly drew out each word, still not looking at Sheila. "I love seeing him get all sweaty and nervous over the things I tell him. Giving him the lurid details of my life is like turning a fat, pig-body on a spit. I can watch him tremble and see his eyes sizzling in his fat head. I can practically taste the bile rising in his throat. One of these days I just know I'm going to make him puke. And today might have been the day—I had something special for him." Trent turned and gave Sheila the demonic grin that never failed to excite and frighten her at the same time. Trent used words as weapons, brandishing their sharp edges as if they were a fencer's blade. Sheila watched him warily. She didn't know what to say. Angering Trent was even worse than upsetting her father. She searched for something to redeem herself, but could think of nothing. "Forget it," Trent spat, letting her off the hook. "Being your therapist is almost as good. So what's going on?"

Feeling relieved, Sheila crossed the room to Trent's bed, sat beneath the winged dragon, and began to tell him about the previous night.

WHAT CAUSES EMOTIONAL DISTURBANCE?

Emotional disturbance is usually the result of many complicated, interlinking factors. The factors that contribute to an individual's likelihood of developing emotional disturbance are
called risk factors. Some of the most common risk factors are:

- *The individual's personal characteristics*. Risk factors in
  this category might include personality,
  temperament, intelligence, history of mental illness,
  genetic makeup, and whether the person has a high
  or low tolerance for stress.
- *Caregiver functioning and ability*. Parents, guardians,
  and other caregivers play an **integral** role in children's
  emotional development. Parents struggling with issues
  like substance abuse, mental health concerns, and
  employment difficulties may cause or compound
  emotional disturbances in their children.
- *Family functioning, dynamics, and support systems*.
  How well a family communicates, the forms of
  discipline used within a family, the existence of
  neglect or abuse, interpersonal relationships between
  individual family members, and other dynamics within
  the home will impact a child's emotional development
  and may be a risk factor for emotional disturbance.
  Furthermore, having a strong support network within
  the family consisting of different people who the
  young person can turn to for guidance and
  understanding can be an important defense against
  developing emotional difficulties.
- **Peer** *relations*. The family is an important
  environmental and **developmental** influence on
  children, but children's peers also have a tremendous
  impact on shaping a young person's reality. Bullying
  and rejection by peers puts young people at a greatly

increased risk of developing emotional disturbance. Close association with peers who are themselves experiencing emotional disturbance or who are engaged in reckless or criminal behavior also puts young people at risk for developing emotional disturbance themselves.

- *School performance.* For the majority of youth, the greatest quantity of time spent outside the home is spent in school. Poor performance and negative experiences at school greatly impact a young person's self-esteem and emotional development. Poor school performance can be both a risk factor for and a sign of emotional disturbance. On the other hand, positive school experiences and performance can help a young person through emotionally difficult times.
- *Neighborhood characteristics.* The stresses, fears, and negative influences that often come with living in high crime or **impoverished** areas can increase the chances of youth developing emotional disturbance.

We have already seen Sheila display some of the characteristics of emotional disturbance. In chapter 1, she exhibited an inability to control her anger, had an emotional reaction far out of proportion with the circumstances she encountered, and displayed antisocial behavior. In chapter 2, we also see that her grades are slipping and that she is skipping school.

In addition to the characteristics of emotional disturbance that Sheila displays, we see some of the risk factors for emotional disturbance present in her life. Based on her father's inability to communicate and adequately address his daughter's behavior, we may suspect that her caregiver's functioning (number two in the list of emotional disturbance risk factors) and her family's functioning, dynamics, and support systems (number three on the list) are placing her at

A young person with an emotional disturbance may retreat into his own world.

Sheila, like many other adolescents with an emotional disturbance, chooses a certain "look" that reflects her inner turmoil.

risk. Furthermore, through the description of bullying that Sheila records in her journal, we see that Sheila's peer relations (number four on the list) are a risk factor affecting her emotional well-being. Her relationship with Trent also appears to be a risk factor.

Like Sheila, Trent displays both characteristics of and risk factors for emotional disturbance. He exhibits highly antisocial behavior and seems to live within bizarre family dynamics. His parents appear to be negligent, and the writing Trent displays upon his wall indicates he has suffered from physical abuse. Many factors can contribute to emotional disturbance, but parental neglect and abuse are some of the chief causes of emotional disturbance in young people.

Young people who externalize their emotional problems may be labeled as troublemakers.

INTERNALIZING AND EXTERNALIZING BEHAVIORS

When teachers or health-care professionals watch for signs of emotional disturbance, they look for both internalizing and externalizing behaviors. Internalizing behaviors are behaviors in which an individual withdraws and keeps her disturbing emotions inside. Externalizing behaviors are behaviors in which an individual acts out, turning her internal turmoil into external disruptive behaviors.

Most people with emotional disturbance will display some of each type of behavior, often acting differently depending upon the environment. For example, at school a teen may appear to have internalized behavior. She bottles up her emotions when she is targeted for ridicule by her peers. At home, however, she displays externalized behaviors as she releases her anger by starting fights with her siblings or yelling at her parents.

An individual with externalizing behaviors appears to behave in the opposite manner. At home, he may withdraw into his room. At school, however, he seems to act out. This individual may be externalizing his behaviors at school by provoking teachers and other school staff. Sometimes young people with emotional disturbance who are externalizing are wrongly labeled as "troublemakers," "problem kids," or "bad apples." People may think these students simply need harsh discipline to correct their behavior. Many teachers and school officials, however, are trained to recognize such behaviors as clues that the child is in need of help rather than in need of punishment.

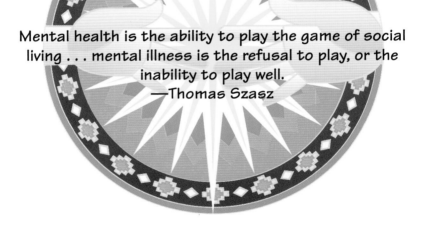

Mental health is the ability to play the game of social living . . . mental illness is the refusal to play, or the inability to play well.
—Thomas Szasz

3

THE TRUTH AS HE SEES IT

Sheila sat on Trent's bed, its rusty springs creaking with her every movement, and told him the story of the previous night. When she described how she had overturned her dresser, smashed her lamp, and thrown glass jars of paint against the wall, Trent smiled with approval. When she expressed her sorrow and regret, Trent scowled. Sheila shrank from his look. She hated to disappoint him. But when he spoke, it was in a smoky, soothing voice, the type of voice one uses for persuasion. He kneeled before Sheila as she sat on the bed.

"So why are you upset, Sheila? What do you think you did wrong?" He began his questions. It was a ritual with them. Sheila would go to Trent with her troubling emotions. He would ask her about her feelings, and then he'd tell her why she was wrong, what the truth was behind her emotions, and thus banish the troubling doubts that gnawed at her mind.

"I'm upset because I got so angry for no reason," she replied obediently.

"Why does getting angry upset you?" Trent questioned like an expert psychiatrist.

"Because I hurt my dad. Because he didn't do anything wrong, and I hurt his feelings," Sheila answered. She knew this wouldn't be an acceptable excuse for Trent, but the ritual was important.

"Why does it matter if you hurt his feelings?" Trent pushed her further. Sheila thought about it for a moment. It seemed like a stu-

39

pid question, and yet suddenly she wasn't quite sure what her answer should be.

"Well, because he loves me . . . because he wants what's best for me," she replied hesitantly.

"Aha!" Trent's eyes narrowed. He placed one hand on each side of Sheila's knees and leaned forward. "See, that's where you're wrong, Sheila. That's what they always use to get us. We should act the way they want because they love us?! Give me a break." Trent expelled the words like bitter food from his mouth, and Sheila ate readily, starving for anything that would relieve her guilt. "Love is selfish. People don't have kids because they love them. They have kids out of selfishness, because they want to feel like they have a purpose, because they want to feel like they're doing something with their pathetic, meaningless lives. They don't want to give love; they want to receive love." Trent raised himself up, leaned closer to Sheila's face, pierced her eyes with his stare, and lowered his voice to a whisper. "Or they want kids to fulfill some sick need or desire." For a moment the words caught in his throat, nearly revealing weakness, but he forced the bile down and spoke with new vengeance. "And when they're inevitably disappointed, what do they do? They sit in front of the television all day, or they drink themselves to death, or they *run away*." Trent emphasized his last words with a viciousness that made Sheila's emotions boil anew.

She thought about her mother. Trent was right. That's exactly what parents did. They had kids for stupid, selfish reasons, and then when the kids weren't what the parents had expected, they just ran away, just like her mom. Why shouldn't she be angry? Why shouldn't she throw fits and destroy things? She didn't owe anyone anything. She especially didn't owe her father. Why did she care how he felt? He practically drove away her mother.

❖❖

Trent watched closely as Sheila's face contorted in reaction to his words. He felt like he'd known these truths from the moment he was born. By now, he believed himself too bitter to feel any sorrow, but Sheila, he realized, was new to the facts. She still became angry, then tearful. Trent knew about Sheila's mother, about how she had packed up one day, declared that everyone was holding her back, that getting married and having kids was the worst decision she'd ever made, about how she'd walked out saying she was sick of being stifled, that she was going to go be something. He knew Sheila was thinking about this too. He watched as the anger melted like hot wax down her face and oozed into painful tears. He couldn't tolerate tears. Anger was power. Tears were dangerous. He needed to teach her to be hard, to survive, to become numb.

As Sheila began to cry, Trent stood, towered over her for a moment so she could feel his presence, and then sat beside her. He put a thin arm about her quaking shoulders and reached with his other hand into his pocket. "I've got something that will make you feel better." He withdrew his fist and uncurled his fingers to reveal a small pocketknife nestled in his palm. He expertly flicked it open and held it toward Sheila. The blade glowed like honey in the basement's orange light. "Find the hurt and cut it out," Trent whispered.

Sheila's pulse quickened at the sight of the blade. It looked delicate and mesmerizing in Trent's wizard-like fingertips. It seemed as if the painted dragon that loomed with spread wings above them held its breath as Sheila reached for Trent's offering. The knife was surprisingly heavy for its size. Sheila's head swarmed with the emotions Trent had unleashed, and the knife's weight in her fingertips felt like strength, like ground, like something to hold on to. Trent watched Sheila, hardly breathing. They were standing on a cliff together, and she was about to carry them over the edge. Sheila felt the tension growing, pitching within her as she pulled a tattered sleeve back to reveal her forearm. She lowered the blade to her wrist: Trent reached for her hand.

"No," he whispered. "Not where they can see it." He ran his fingers gently up her arm and pulled her sleeve to her shoulder. "Here," he said, brushing the soft flesh above her elbow.

Sheila looked at the delicate rivers of blue-green veins that laced beneath her translucent skin. Then, with deliberate slowness, she drew a thin line with the blade. It was surprisingly sharp, and her skin parted effortlessly, revealing the pink flesh below. For a moment, there was no blood, just perfectly parted skin separated by a simple, beautifully surgical, pink line. Everything hung on the brink of that vibrant, painless moment. And then the liquid dots appeared, welled, flowed, and all Sheila's emotions broke over the dam and washed away in the sudden flood of red. She watched emotionless, fascinated and numb, as the crimson blood coursed in streams down the gradual slope of her arm. She felt Trent lift the knife from her fingertips, and she watched as Trent cut his own flesh.

STRUGGLING WITH EMOTIONAL DISTURBANCE

A person suffering from emotional disturbance may look for ways to **rationalize** her behavior. Like many people, both Sheila and Trent use anger to protect themselves from other, more painful emotions like sadness and despair. However, losing control and yelling at her father makes Sheila feel terrible. She doesn't want to hurt her father with her outbursts, but she does not know how to control her anger. To ease the pain her outbursts cause, Sheila looks for reasons and excuses that will make her actions seem okay. She turns to Trent for an explanation of her behavior that will **absolve** her of responsibility and guilt.

When two friends both experience emotional problems, they may reinforce each other's warped perspectives.

In an attempt to understand and cope with the pain he has experienced in his own life, Trent has developed a view of the world in which he and Sheila are victims of other people's selfishness and inadequacies. According to Trent's view, if he and Sheila display anger or violence, other people are to blame. Listening to Trent allows Sheila to forget her guilt. The type of disrupted thinking Trent displays, consisting of an illogical thought progression or irrational assumptions (for instance, based upon his own negative experiences, he assumes that parents only have children for selfish reasons and that this injustice allows children to behave in any manner they wish) is the type of thinking that can be a sign of emotional disturbance. Cognitive therapy with a psychiatrist or other mental health professional would seek to explore and correct this dysfunctional thinking.

At the same time that Trent makes Sheila feel justified in her anger, he also unearths one of the causes of Sheila's emotional disturbance, thus unleashing new pain. Sheila and Trent do, in fact, appear to be the victims of others' abandonment, neglect, and abuse. Although we do not know the precise circumstances surrounding her mother's departure, we can see that this loss has created deep hurt, anger, and resentment in Sheila's life. Similarly, we do not know the details of the abuse that Trent has suffered, but we can see that it has led him to develop a bitterly **cynical** worldview, to use anger as a method of protecting himself from more painful emotions, and to lose the ability to trust other people.

Trent's reactions of cynicism, anger, and mistrust are some of the most common reactions felt by young people who have been physically and emotionally abused and are frequently occurring features of emotional disturbance. In cases like Sheila's and Trent's, it sometimes takes years of working with a qualified professional such as a psychiatrist, psychologist, counselor, or social worker, to overcome the

Although peers can help relieve some of the loneliness and anguish of an emotional disturbance, an unhealthy relationship can also lead to increased symptoms.

feelings of anger and mistrust that have become tools of survival.

Diagnosis and Treatment

Parents are supposed to be the people children can count on for love, support, security, and safety. But where are children like Sheila and Trent supposed to turn when their parents can't or won't provide the love, support, and guidance their children need? Where would you turn if your parents were neglecting, harming, or simply didn't know how to help you?

Providing support, care, and guidance to children is one of the most important roles schools play in our society. Schools are places of education, but a complete education goes far beyond the lessons that happen in the classroom. Many children find that when something is wrong at home or when they have a problem they don't know how to deal with, their school is the place they can turn for help.

Many professionals, both inside and outside the school setting, are trained to recognize signs of emotional disturbance in young people. Teachers, nurses, doctors, school counselors, and social workers are just some of the people who watch for characteristics of and risk factors for emotional disturbance in the lives of young people. Educators need training in recognizing signs of emotional disturbance because it can sometimes be more difficult to recognize than other special needs like physical or learning disabilities. Serious emotional disturbance may in certain cases go undetected for a long time. For example, a young person may live in social isolation with no one aware of what is going on within the young person's home. Many young people, not wanting their teachers or friends to know that anything is wrong, become very *adept* at hiding their true experiences and emotions and may not immediately appear to

Many school professionals are trained to recognize the symptoms of emotional disturbance.

observers to be at high risk. Parents may notice signs that something is wrong, but not know how to respond. Or, worse yet, many parents, teachers, and other adults may disregard signs of emotional disturbance in young people, thinking that the disturbing behaviors are just part of child-ish misbehavior, teenage *angst*, or rebellion.

Within the school setting, thanks to the legal guarantees found within IDEA (discussed in chapter 1), a child who is determined to have emotional disturbance is entitled to the services he needs to help him handle the school learning en-

A student who has an emotional disturbance is entitled to special services. These may include counseling or an adapted learning environment. Often, he will receive one-on-one attention from counselors, school psychologists, or special education teachers.

Schools are required to provide services to a student who has been determined to have an emotional disturbance until he graduates or reaches the age of twenty-one.

vironment. This is achieved through a very specific process defined within IDEA. *All* preschool and school-age students, regardless of the severity of their disability, must be provided an "appropriate education" in the "least restrictive environment." Teachers, school psychologists, other school staff, and the child's parents will form a team to examine the student's needs as well as her eligibility for special services (according to IDEA, only students who meet specific special needs criteria can be eligible to the services that state and federal funds provide). This team will then create something called an individualized education plan (IEP) to develop a program that meets that student's specific needs. To insure that the educational program is appropriate to the child's current (and evolving) needs, IEP programs must be reviewed at least annually, with periodic reevaluations conducted at least every three years.

CONDUCT DISORDER

You will often hear emotional disturbance referred to as a conduct disorder. According to the *Diagnostic and Statistical Manual of Mental Disorders,* fourth edition (DSM-IV), the book of criteria that doctors use to diagnose psychiatric illnesses, a conduct disorder is a "repetitive and persistent behavior in which the basic rights of others or major age-appropriate social norms or rules are violated." In other words, when a person has a conduct disorder, he acts in unacceptable ways and disrespects other people. For example, a child who is always breaking rules at school, taking things from other children, and yelling at his teacher or other

A child with a conduct disorder often fails to feel remorse after misbehavior.

Frequent episodes of fighting may be a symptom of a conduct disorder.

A child with a conduct disorder will have difficulty getting along with others, both at home and at school.

adults might be suffering from conduct disorder (or emotional disturbance). As many as six percent of all school-age children, or six out of every one hundred, may have conduct disorder. Three to four times more boys are diagnosed with conduct disorder than girls, and more adolescents appear to suffer from conduct disorder than younger children.

Some warning signs of conduct disorder and emotional disturbance include violence (such as fighting, destroying things, showing cruelty to people and animals, and forcing others into unwanted sexual acts), lying, being extremely impulsive, skipping school, running away from home, lacking empathy for other people, and failing to feel remorse after doing something wrong or hurtful to others. To be diagnosed with conduct disorder, these symptoms must begin before the individual turns eighteen.

Case Study

Alex, a twelve-year-old boy with conduct disorder, was constantly disrupting class and endangering his fellow classmates. He talked loudly whenever the teacher talked, argued and yelled when the teacher tried to discipline him, stole items from his classmates on an almost daily basis, and even occasionally bit classmates when he got angry—a behavior not uncommon among young children, but hugely inappropriate for a child of Alex's age.

When Alex's school psychologist examined the situation, she found that Alex displayed his disruptive behavior not only in school, but at home as well. His mother, a single parent of four children, found it nearly impossible to control Alex's behavior, especially while trying to care for his three younger siblings. Alex's mother often resorted to bribes and negotiating with Alex in an attempt to control his behavior. The school psychologist found this happening in a number of Alex's classrooms as well—teachers exhausted and frustrated from trying to control Alex would rely on pleading with him and offering him rewards like extra minutes at recess in exchange for good behavior. Although these tactics sometimes gave Alex's mother and teachers a few extra moments of peace, in the long run they only served to reinforce his negative behavior by teaching him that he would get rewarded for acting out. Additionally, the punishments they gave, which usually consisted of making him leave class or sit alone at the back of the room, also served to reinforce his behavior by teaching Alex that if he misbehaved he would get out of doing his work.

The school psychologist began to treat Alex by providing "management training" to his mother and teachers. In this training, the psychologist met with Alex's mother and teach-

A time-out period may not be an appropriate consequence for misbehavior if it means the child gets to retreat to his room and escape doing chores.

Rewards that include favorite activities can encourage appropriate behaviors in a child with a conduct disorder.

ers and discussed ways to behave differently toward Alex. The psychologist taught Alex's mother and teachers to resist the frustration that caused them to give in to Alex's negative behaviors, to reinforce his positive behaviors with praise and rewards, and to discourage negative behaviors with mild punishment. Typical punishments for misbehavior now centered around losing privileges like recess, having to eat lunch at his desk, and having to complete additional homework assignments, which often consisted of lessons on empathy and respecting others. In the "training groups," Alex's teachers also created a support network and made plans for how they would help each other when Alex got out of hand. Alex's mother found that meeting with his teachers helped her feel supported in her struggle to deal with her son.

When a behavior management plan is first implemented, the child will not immediately respond in a positive manner. She may initially feel resentful, bored, or frustrated.

A child who has learned to manage his behavior will get along better at school and at home.

For a time after this new plan was implemented, Alex's behavior appeared to get even worse as he fiercely resisted his teachers' and mother's attempts to gain control. However, with each other's support, his teachers and mother refused to give in to his frustrating behavior, and after one year, Alex was showing improvement in school. He was still often argumentative, but his grades had improved, he interrupted class less frequently, and he had stopped harming and stealing from other children, behavior that carried the most unpleasant punishment.

OPPOSITIONAL DEFIANT DISORDER

Children with emotional disturbance are also often diagnosed as having oppositional defiant disorder. Oppositional defiant disorder is very similar to conduct disorder in that the child behaves disobediently. However, a child with oppositional defiant disorder does not violate the rights of other people the way many children with conduct disorder do. The DSM-IV says that a child with oppositional defiant disorder has "a recurrent pattern of negativistic, defiant, disobedient, and hostile behavior toward authority figures that persists for at least six months."

A child with oppositional defiant disorder will usually display at least four behaviors such as being spiteful or vindictive, losing his temper, arguing with adults or authority figures, refusing to follow rules set by adults, doing things to purposefully annoy or upset other people, and blaming his behavior and failures on other people.

Children with oppositional defiant disorders often appear hostile, particularly to authority figures.

Like conduct disorder, oppositional defiant disorder is experienced by boys and adolescents more frequently than by girls and younger children. Also like other forms of emotional disturbance, conditions within the child's family environment are often the main cause of the disorder. All children are disobedient, defiant, or push behavioral boundaries sometimes, but for children with oppositional defiant disorder and emotional disturbance, something in their environment (like physical abuse or lack of proper discipline) is causing them to develop social and emotional maladjustments.

Sometimes parents, teachers, friends, and others find children with emotional disturbances like oppositional defiant and conduct disorder difficult to tolerate. They may find that the child tries their patience and causes them stress. However, a child with an emotional disturbance is experiencing just as much, and usually more, emotional distress as he is causing to those around him.

Case Study

Clara, a ten-year-old girl, had never seriously misbehaved at home until she entered the fifth grade. Then, she suddenly seemed like a different child. She was generally quiet and well behaved—until a teacher asked her to perform a task like reading aloud or writing something on the blackboard. Then Clara became absolutely defiant, not only refusing to complete the teacher's request, but arguing and throwing temper tantrums as well. Clara soon began displaying this behavior at home as well, throwing temper tantrums when she was told to do her homework and refusing to obey household rules. Her grades, which had been average before, fell sharply. At first both her teachers and parents assumed Clara was just going through a difficult phase related to approaching adolescence, and that she would adjust and

An adolescent's oppositional defiant disorder may be dismissed as typical teenage moodiness.

return to her former, well-behaved self. However, Clara's behavior became steadily worse for eight months, at which time Clara's parents requested that she be evaluated by the school psychologist.

When referred to the school psychologist for testing, Clara was diagnosed with oppositional defiant disorder. Because her defiance and tantrums seemed to be triggered by requests to perform schoolwork, the psychologist suspected that Clara might have some undiagnosed learning disabilities that were interfering with her ability to do work and creating frustration that fueled her misbehavior. By performing certain tests, the psychologist found that his suspicion was correct. Clara had dyslexia, a learning disability that made it difficult for Clara to read. In earlier grades, Clara had adapted to her classroom environment and developed ways to hide her learning difficulties. However, the more difficult material she encountered in fifth grade made it impossible to hide her inability to do the work, so she had developed a system of misbehaving as a new disguise for her learning disability.

Clara began spending time each day with a special education teacher who gave her extra help in learning to read and manage her dyslexia. She also met once each week with her school psychologist to address continuing behavioral and emotional difficulties. After just three months, Clara was already showing a marked improvement in her reading abilities and her behavior.

Addiction is . . . cunning and powerful.
—Erica Jong

4

BLOODLETTING

That night, back in her apartment, Sheila carefully extracted a blade from one of her father's razors. Unlike Trent's weighty pocketknife, the razor blade was thin and delicate, barely a breath of metal. Nevertheless, it hummed with secret promise in her hand. She carefully wrapped the silver instrument in newspaper to protect it.

The next morning, as she dressed for school, Sheila slid the wrapped blade into her sock so she could feel its calming presence against her ankle. In the coming weeks, the razor blade became Sheila's best friend. She carried it everywhere. It was a tiny piece of power that no one knew she had. When she felt the inner turmoil rising, she took a hall pass to the bathroom. Standing in the white-tiled room, she placed a foot on the toilet seat, extracted the secret package from where it pulsed against her ankle, carefully un-wrapped the newspaper, and pulled forth her friend. If she was wearing her army pants, she rolled them up to expose her calf. If wearing her paint-splattered dresses, she pulled the hem up past her knee, then cut a clean line across the inside of her thigh. She savored the exquisite release that came with every cut and watched as the red droplets chased each other down her skin and dripped into the water below, staining it pink.

What began as an intriguing novelty soon became a daily method of survival. She cut when people called her "freak." She cut instead of picking fights with her sister. When anger rose in response to her father's presence, she locked herself in her bedroom and cut with ferocious purpose. When she visited Trent, they cut together just for fun. And sometimes, late at night, Sheila took a photograph from the bottom of her dresser drawer. Staring at her mother's smiling face, Sheila sliced six parallel incisions in her upper arm, one for each year her mother had been gone.

As the weeks progressed, thin white scars appeared like bundles of matchsticks on Sheila's skin. She loved these scars almost as much as the cuts that had born them. Every scar was a story. She no longer wrote vicious lines of poetry. Instead, she calmly carved the story of her pain on her skin. Soon, cutting was an art form, the one thing that Sheila felt she could control, the one thing that gave her power. When the school hallways brought their insults, Sheila could not limit how much they would hurt. When memories of her mother stirred, Sheila could not prevent the inner turmoil they would rouse. But when she cut, Sheila was in perfect control. She wielded the blade like an expert conductor directing an orchestra with his wand. Like the conductor, Sheila alone had the power to say how loud, how slow, how long, how deep the blade's music would play.

As Sheila perfected her cutting technique, she seemed to be perfecting the *facade* with which she lived her life as well. Soon, it became almost easy to act normal again, to quell rising anger when it threatened, to have a conversation with her father that didn't end in mindless destruction, to speak with her sister without ripping into the little girl's feelings, to walk head high through the school hallways and barely hear the insults cast her way. Now, any emotion that needed release ended not by losing herself in rage but by shedding blood.

On the surface, things appeared to be changing. Sheila felt powerful and in control. Turning the newspaper-wrapped blade over between her fingers, she watched her classmates and teachers smugly. They had no idea what she could do, the strength that she had. But somewhere deep inside, Sheila sensed that this newfound happiness was a lie, a lie she could only believe in until the final drop of blood dried on her skin. Then, as the relief passed, realization would dawn. She was cutting herself—deliberately forcing a razor blade into her skin! Sheila tried to convince herself otherwise, but she had the gnawing sense that the cutting was a deception, an illusion, a diversion to draw her attention away from the things that were too painful to acknowledge. She lived in twilight days filled with deepening shadows. Sheila sensed she was spiraling down a new rabbit hole of danger. Soon it took larger cuts and more blood to give her the same feeling of release that a simple incision had brought before. Though on the surface she felt calmer than she had in years, deep down Sheila knew that each strike of the blade made the rabbit hole grow deeper.

During this spiraling descent, Sheila met Mara, and yet another turmoil was unleashed inside Sheila. Mara had olive-dark skin, deep black hair, and made Sheila doubt everything she had ever believed about herself. She first met Mara at a coffee shop where Sheila had intended to see a ***poetry slam***, a place where poets gave dramatic, prop- and costume-laden performances of their work. She arrived and found Mara's band beating on dented instruments instead. This was infinitely disappointing. Sheila hated listening to her peers' ***grunge*** bands—the groups that claimed to be deep and artistic, but were really just Nirvana wanna-be's minus the thought and the talent. But as she began watching the performance, Sheila hardly even noticed how terrible the band was. Mara's gravelly voice was so interesting it didn't matter what the rest of the music sounded like.

After the performance, as Mara packed up her microphone and guitar, Sheila approached.

"Hey, your band's terrible but you're really good." Sheila couldn't believe what she was hearing herself say. What was she doing? Was she an idiot? Not only was she going up and talking to this stranger, she was obviously trying to offend her as well. Mara whirled around, her black hair swishing.

"I know." Mara smiled.

Sheila didn't think she needed a friend. Trent was all she needed. But something about Mara made her want to change her mind.

SELF-CUTTING AND SELF-HARM

Like most people, you probably try to avoid pain as much as possible. After all, it hurts! It may be difficult, then, to understand why someone would hurt himself on purpose. Doctors once thought that self-cutting was a rare form of suicidal behavior. Recent studies, however, have shown that self-cutting and other forms of self-harm (also referred to as self-injury, self-mutilation, auto-aggression, and many other terms) are neither rare nor **exhibitions** of suicidal desires. Many people experiencing emotional disturbance turn to self-injury not to attempt suicide but to attempt finding relief.

It may seem strange to think that a person with emotional pain would inflict physical harm upon himself in order to make himself feel better, but many people who engage in self-injury say that it helps them to gain control of their overwhelming emotions. Many people who purposefully injure themselves claim that they cannot control their tumultuous emotions, but they *can* control the cuts they make on their skin. Other people who cut themselves say that the effect is largely symbolic, that they are creating an opening in their physical bodies to let out their inner pain and turmoil. As another explanation of their practice, some people who self-cut say that when depression and other emotional trauma make them feel "dead" inside, cutting and seeing their blood reminds them that they are alive. For these people, cutting, far from being an attempt at suicide, is an attempt to reconnect with life. Still other people speculate that self-injury is a cry for help—a way to make their inner anguish visible to the world so that someone will see their hurt and come to their aid.

No matter what the explanation, cutting appears to be a coping mechanism for dealing with one's emotional disturbance. However, this does not mean that cutting is a safe, healthy, or successful coping method. Self-injury is a very dangerous behavior. Many people who self-cut describe themselves as becoming addicted to their cutting behavior. Over time the individual needs to make bigger and deeper cuts to get the same feeling that a smaller cut previously gave her. This is similar to what an alcoholic experiences— needing to have more and more alcohol to achieve the same feeling that less alcohol gave her before. (In fact, substance abuse is also very common among people with emotional disturbance.) Similar to an alcoholic or other addict's behavior, many people who self-cut find their actions spinning out of control. Suddenly, the thing that had made them feel powerful has power over them. Unable to stop the behavior, the person may begin to feel weak and helpless. These negative feelings toward themselves push them deeper into their emotional disturbance, which in turn

forces them to cut themselves even more, thus creating a descending cycle of self-abuse.

Fortunately, much research is currently being conducted on self-mutilation, its causes, and its treatments. More and more health professionals are becoming acquainted with the realities of this behavior and are better equipped to help self-injurers. Furthermore, in recent years there have been numerous books about self-injury, and the Internet has allowed many people who injure themselves to join in educational and support networks that help them understand, confront, and overcome their behaviors.

Ninety percent of our lives is governed by emotions.
—Alfred North Whitehead

5

DETECTED

Sheila and Mara had exchanged numbers at the coffee shop. They went to a poetry slam, where Mara listened to Sheila's angry poems, and then Sheila went to see another one of Mara's performances. Their friendship blossomed quickly, and Sheila felt drunk with joy. But, as with all the good feelings Sheila was lucky enough to stumble on, there was an unpleasant side to the joy as well.

When her mother had left their family, Sheila had pulled away from everyone, especially other females. She detested girls with long flowing hair, perfectly manicured fingernails, and carefully applied makeup. She was disgusted by their extreme femininity; she herself preferred boots and army pants, or dresses that were black, tattered, and covered with paint and clay. She couldn't relate to other girls' conversations and concerns. Yet here was Mara, certainly nothing like the Barbie™-doll cheerleaders Sheila hated, but beautiful and feminine nonetheless.

Adding to the confusion, in total contrast to her normal reactions to women, Sheila found herself longing to be more like Mara—to be beautiful like her, confident like her, graceful and womanly with Mara's perfect smile. Standing next to Mara, Sheila felt small, ugly, sick, and disturbed. She ached for just a little bit of Mara's perfection to rub off. Soon she found herself writing sickly-sweet poetry in her dark book in place of the gnashing, bloody words she usually dug into the pages. This was perhaps the most disturbing development of all. Sheila could not make any sense of her feelings.

To make matters worse, Mara seemed oblivious to everything going on in Sheila's mind. She laughed and chatted as though she assumed that she and Sheila were on the same wavelength. Sheila stammered over her own words, but Mara never seemed to notice. In fact, Mara seemed to love to hear Sheila talk. She was always asking Sheila to share her thoughts on an issue or to read some of her poetry. The more time they spent together, the more Sheila feared that someday Mara would find out who Sheila truly was—that she carried rage inside of her, that she threw screaming fits at her father, that she cut herself behind closed doors. Soon, nothing in the world was more important to Sheila than ensuring that Mara did not discover her dark secrets. She even tried to resist the urge to cut. When the desire to cut swelled over her, Sheila concentrated on Mara's face, thought about how kind and "normal" Mara seemed, convinced herself that Mara would be horrified by cutting. Thoughts like these were Sheila's barrier against the rising tide of frustration, confusion, and anger that swept the razor blade into her fingers and washed the sharp edge toward her waiting skin. Sometimes the barrier held, but usually, despite Sheila's attempts to hold them back, the emotions broke over the wall and flooded her mind, drowning her with their power. Sheila struggled in the whirlpool of sorrow until she laid hold of the razor blade, cut through her emotions, and drank the pure air again. Then, like a guilty child eating stolen candy, Sheila tucked the razor blade away, vowed to never use it again, and put on a happy face for Mara.

Sheila had been spending so much time with her new friend that she'd hardly spoken with Trent in weeks. She hadn't gone to his house at all. He didn't seem to care. He didn't even ask Sheila where she'd been or request that she stop by, and Sheila was too busy to notice his withdrawal. But an event one school morning brought Trent suddenly back into focus in Sheila's life.

The high school administration had decided to install metal detectors at the school's front entrance. The first day the metal detectors were in place, they beeped a warning as Trent stepped through their industrial frame. Of course, the metal detectors were beeping for everyone as the students, unaccustomed to such things at school, walked through with buttons on their bags and car keys in their pockets. Teachers were milling around, calmly instructing the students to empty their pockets, remove the items, take note of what they could not bring in the future. No one seemed alarmed when Trent set off the metal detector. When he was ordered to empty his pockets, however, Trent blatantly refused. Watching the exchange, Sheila knew what no one else did—that Trent had his knife in his pocket, and he wasn't about to give it up. After a lengthy standoff with the football coach, who was overseeing the metal detectors' first run, the security guard pulled Trent over to the wall and started patting him down.

At the older man's touch, Trent's face went white. Sheila watched in horror as Trent appeared to turn inside out. His eyes caved inward. His chest began to heave. Sheila heard an animal-like growl start in Trent's throat, and she knew something terrible was about to happen. Then the security guard touched Trent's leg, and Trent went berserk. His leg shot back in a reflexive kick that landed squarely on the security guard's jaw. The security guard's head snapped, his teeth closing with a sharp click, and he stumbled backward to the floor. The principal and football coach leapt forward to seize Trent. Sheila saw the metal glinting in Trent's hand and knew that he'd already extracted and opened the knife with lightning speed. Book bags fell around the hallway like apples from trees as students raced to see the scuffle.

The sudden crush of bodies blocked Sheila's view, but she could hear Trent screaming, "Don't touch me! I'll kill you if you touch me!" His voice sounded like it wasn't his own.

Panic welled in Sheila's stomach as she pushed and dodged around the other students in an attempt to see her friend. Through the jostling shoulders and craning necks, she caught glimpses of the struggle. Both the principal and the football coach had their arms locked around Trent, keeping Trent's own arms pinned to his side, but he twisted, squirmed, and kicked like a rabid animal. Sheila thought she saw Trent bite the principal's arm. Flashes of red appeared on the football coach's hands where he had been slashed by Trent's knife. The whole time, Trent kept growling and screaming, "I'll kill you! I'll kill you! Don't touch me! I'll kill you!"

And then, without warning, everything stopped. Trent's body went limp as a rag doll's. It was as if he'd been an electronic toy and someone had simply pulled his plug. He hung lifeless in the men's arms, his head lolling back, his eyes staring open at the ceiling but not appearing to see anything at all. Sheila didn't understand what had happened, but she suddenly felt like she also might crack. Teachers and security guards were ushering students every which way. An ambulance was called, and through the chaos, Sheila saw Trent being loaded through its doors.

As soon as the emergency vehicle pulled away, Sheila rushed into the closest bathroom, locked the stall door behind her, and cut herself eight times in a row.

WHAT IS A PSYCHOTIC EPISODE?

A psychotic episode is a period of time in which an individual loses touch with reality, suffers from **delusions**, and may even experience hallucinations. The individual may become violent as he attempts to protect himself from the delusions or hallucinations. Psychotic episodes may be part of a larger psychiatric disorder, may occur as the result of using substances like intoxicants or certain medications, or may occur because something in the present triggers a reliving of a traumatic event from the past.

From the situation Sheila viewed, one would suspect that Trent's psychotic episode occurs because he is reliving something from his past. Trent is already stressed at the thought of having his pocketknife, the thing he uses for emotional strength and protection, taken away. When the security guard touches Trent's leg, Trent appears to separate from reality. It is very likely that he does this because the security guard's touch reminds Trent of some form of physical abuse he suffered in the past. Trent appears not only to be reminded of the abuse, however, but to actually be transported back into the experience, which he relives in front of Sheila's (and everyone else's) eyes. This type of flashback is a common feature of people suffering from emotional disturbance as the result of trauma or abuse, and a non-drug-induced psychotic episode is a clear sign of an underlying and serious emotional disturbance.

EMOTIONAL DISTURBANCE IN THE SCHOOL SETTING

There are many types of conditions that may affect young people and cause them to have special needs in the school setting. For example, a child who is hard of hearing would require certain conditions in the classroom, such as being

A child's emotions may be so strong that they get in the way of her learning.

seated in the front of the room where he can hear better and see the teacher's lips, to maximize his ability to understand a lesson. A child with learning disabilities may need to go to individualized classes in which she can have one-on-one help with specific material. Some students may have physical or mental disabilities that interfere with their ability to learn or perform well in school.

In the case of young people with emotional disturbance, it is emotions rather than physical or mental disabilities that interfere with their ability to learn. For example, a child suffering from abuse at home may be filled with such sadness, depression, fear, and emotional trauma that he cannot concentrate while he is at school. In such a case, adults must intervene both to assure that the child is protected from abuse and to make sure that the school setting is appropriate for the child to be able to learn.

Our laws require that no child be left out; each is entitled to the services she needs to learn.

As was discussed in chapter 1, the United States and Canada have laws that guarantee a proper education to all children and that require the special needs of youth be met in the education setting. In the United States, IDEA guarantees a free and "appropriate" education to every child. This means that if a child requires additional educational services because of a special need like emotional disturbance, those services must be provided by the school at no extra cost to the child or the child's family. According to IDEA, schools must take the following steps when determining whether a child has special educational needs.

This child, no matter what his disability, is entitled to a free and "appropriate" education.

1. **Search**: In most cases, a child's special needs are discovered because teachers and/or parents have noticed that the child displays significant learning difficulties and/or behavioral problems. The teachers or parents ask the school psychologist to perform tests that will determine whether the child has a special need.
2. **Find**: If the tests that the school psychologist performs show that the child has a special need, the school psychologist, teachers, and other necessary personnel will collect information about the child and her condition. They will use this information to design a plan for evaluating the student's special needs.
3. **Evaluation**: The school psychologist, teachers, and other personnel will evaluate the child's needs in all areas of her learning environment. This usually involves evaluating the home as well as the school environment. They will use this information to develop an individualized education plan (IEP).
4. **Conference**: The child's parents or guardians will meet with the school psychologist, teachers, and other personnel to discuss the results of the evaluation.
5. **Parents' decision process**: At this stage, parents have a chance to learn about their child's special need, have their questions answered and concerns addressed, and either accept or reject the education plan that has been designed for their child.
6. **Appeals process**: If parents reject the IEP that the school has developed for their child, or if the parents believe the school has given their child an incorrect diagnosis, they can appeal the school's decision first to the school. If they still disagree with the results of the appeal, they can seek further appeals with the county or state governments.
7. **Follow-up**: Every three years, the school psychologist

A student's needs and performance will be reevaluated periodically.

and other involved personnel will reevaluate the child's diagnosis, needs, and individualized education plan. However, if there is a significant change in the child's situation, the parents and/or teachers can request the child be reevaluated sooner. After this re-examination of the child's needs, the parents will once again have a chance to meet with school officials, examine the school's finding, accept or reject the IEP, and appeal the school's decision.

The greatest influence on a child's life comes from his family and home environment. However, the majority of time a young person spends outside of his home, he spends in school. Therefore, a child's school and teachers also have a huge influence on his development. The guidelines laid out by IDEA are meant to create a system in which the parents, teachers, and school work together in the best interests of the child.

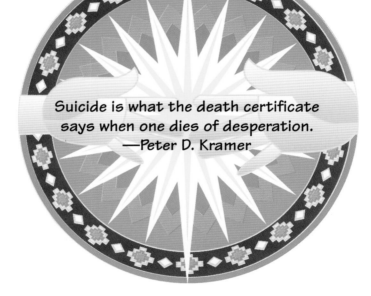

Suicide is what the death certificate
says when one dies of desperation.
—Peter D. Kramer

6

A CUT TOO DEEP

Sheila was sure Trent would be kicked out of school. The day after he went berserk in the halls, she went to the hospital to try to see him, but the hospital staff said he couldn't have any visitors. Though the halls whispered with talk, no one at school could give Sheila any details of what was going on. Most of the students seemed unsurprised—Trent had always been a weird kid. Some of the teachers seemed relieved—Trent had always been a ticking time bomb waiting to go off, and now he was somewhere he couldn't hurt anyone.

Sheila stopped by the hospital twice more with no success. Either they wouldn't allow her to see Trent, or Trent wouldn't let her see him . . . Sheila didn't know which. But a week after the episode, the hospital staff told her Trent had been released. That night, she went to his house, gently pushed open the door, walked past his zombie-parents, and descended into the basement.

All the bare lightbulbs blazed overhead, and Trent sat in his usual position in front of the strange diorama. Something, however, was different about him. His shoulders seemed skinnier. His whole body sagged. He turned and smiled when Sheila approached. The brutality was gone from his grin. Somehow this was not comforting to Sheila. She noted how dead and sad Trent's eyes looked. *What have they done to him?* she wondered. *Where is the anger?* But she knew these were things she could not ask.

"So, I guess you're going to get kicked out of school, huh?" Sheila knew this question would be safe. Trent didn't care about

83

school anyway. Trent turned toward the diorama and carefully adjusted a tree beside a sidewalk.

"Yeah, I guess," he replied listlessly. He paused for a moment and then continued. "They say I don't have to leave, actually."

"Really?" Sheila broke in. This was great news, but Trent didn't look encouraged.

"Yeah, but I'm not going back."

"Why not?" Sheila couldn't believe they were offering Trent another chance and he wasn't going to take it.

"They say that I have to see another counselor, that they want to help me. They say I can't go back unless I agree to get help." The old Trent would have sneered as he said these words, but this shell of Trent seemed void of all emotion. "People have even come by to talk to my parents. Social services is apparently investigating. A lot of good that will do now . . . where were they when I was six?" It was a good question, but Trent didn't act as if he wanted an answer.

Sheila watched her friend, not knowing what to say. She knew she couldn't convince him to return to school, didn't even know if she wanted to. After all, where had school gotten Trent? As if he were reading her thoughts, Trent added, "I sure am going to miss Hambone though." Sheila smiled. This attempt at humor was at least some encouragement.

"Well, look at it this way," Sheila offered, "you'll have plenty of time to finish your diorama." She smiled at Trent and examined his most recent work. "It's really getting close to being done, isn't it?" Trent regarded the diorama as well, but his thoughts seemed to be somewhere else.

"Yeah." His voice carried a hint of something that sounded like relief. "It'll all be done soon." There was something about the way he said it that Sheila didn't like. Trent's words hung heavily around the room, and he suddenly seemed eager to break the silence.

"You wanna smoke?" Trent pulled a bag from his back pocket. It had been a long time since they had smoked pot together . . . probably since before they had started cutting together. "It works a lot better than that medicine they give you at the hospital." Trent smiled. Sheila thought for a moment.

"Yeah," she said finally, "let's get lost together."

The next two weeks were the best Sheila could remember. She went to Trent's house every day after school. They spent long hours in the basement talking and losing themselves in a haze of marijuana smoke. Trent hauled a CD player down to the basement, a luxury he'd never indulged in before, and they listened to pulsing music as they smoked. Sometimes Trent would recite poetry, not the bloody, frightening stuff he and Sheila usually liked, but funny rhymes that delighted her with their senselessness. Something was very different about Trent now. He seemed relaxed, almost happy even. They talked in a way they had never talked before . . . like real friends with something in common other than anger. Sheila told Trent about Mara and all the confusion she was causing in Sheila's life. Trent laughed and told her she was overreacting.

"So you made a new friend, so what?" Trent shrugged so casually, Sheila felt like he could have been a different person. There was no earnestness, no anger, no bizarre philosophizing, just pleasant conversation with no strings attached. Even stranger, Trent seemed to have a lightness, a purpose about him. Sheila was sure it had to do with the diorama, which Trent worked on all day long and which after nearly twelve years was truly nearing completion. Each day now, Sheila looked forward to seeing Trent, not so that he could fan her anger, but so they could smoke pot, lose their anger and pain in its fog, and find the pleasant emotions that were hidden underneath.

That's why it was so shocking when everything fell apart.

Sheila was in English class when Hambone knocked on the door. Sheila saw the counselor and her teacher conversing in whispers, but didn't think anything of it. English was one of the few classes she liked, and it was the only class in which her grades had not recently plummeted. Today they were reading poetry. Sheila felt no need for a distraction. But then the teacher had called her name and asked that she go with Mr. Hammond.

Inwardly, Sheila had rolled her eyes. Getting taken off with Hambone was a significant disgrace . . . it meant you were troubled or "special." *Great*, she thought briefly, *now that they got Trent, they're going to try to weed out all of us.* In the hallway, Mr. Hammond gave Sheila an anxious, pained look but didn't say a thing. He just walked toward his office, and Sheila understood that she should follow.

Sitting in the counselor's office, Sheila had watched with annoyance as Mr. Hammond shuffled papers around on his desk, clearly avoiding Sheila's eyes. She watched as redness crept into the man's face and beads of sweat appeared on his hairless brow. He pushed his glasses up his nose, yanked at his collar with a pudgy finger, and twice cleared his throat. He was making her nervous. Why on earth had he called her in here?

"Sheila, I . . ." he began haltingly. "Sheila, I just don't know how to tell you this." He paused, and Sheila, suddenly very uncomfortable as well, wished he would just get on with it. "Sheila, a team of social workers found Trent in his basement this morning." Mr. Hammond paused again and stared at Sheila, waiting for a reaction. Sheila likewise waited for him to continue, but he did not.

"So?" she finally spoke, the frustration evident in her voice. "He's always in his basement." Mr. Hammond blinked twice, then swallowed hard. Sheila watched the movement roll down his throat and disappear beneath his collar.

"Sheila, they found Trent's body in the basement. Trent committed suicide last night."

Everything shut down. Sheila felt as if someone inside her was flipping every switch to "off." The world went silent, her breathing slowed, and her heart wound down. Mr. Hammond appeared to be getting further and further away as if he were shrinking to a miniature version of himself. The rabbit hole had opened up, and Sheila was slipping over the edge. She needed something, a root, a branch to hold on to, something real to keep her from falling beneath the surface of the earth. She searched Mr. Hammond's faraway face for some clue, some sign, some strength, anything she could grab on to and hold. Then she saw it . . . a tear on Mr. Hammond's cheek. There was something about the strangeness of it, the sheer absurdity of the single tear rolling down the guidance counselor's face that captured Sheila's mind and pulled her back to reality. Like a generator gearing up in a blackout, her body began to hum, her veins began to pulse, and her senses began to return.

As she revived, Mr. Hammond and his single tear growing larger in her vision, Sheila heard a terrible sound. It was the sound of someone laughing, cackling really, unbridled, irreverent guffawing. *Who could possibly be laughing?* she wondered in horror. *Who would laugh at a time like this?* Mr. Hammond appeared to be wondering the same thing, for a look of confusion, perhaps even panic, had come over his face, and he leaned toward Sheila as if he might need to smother her. As he stared, Sheila realized with horror where the laughter was coming from—it was coming from her. Had the whole world gone mad? Hambone was crying, she was laughing, and Trent was dead? Like a train running out of control, laughter careened from her throat, and she was powerless to stop it.

SUBSTANCE ABUSE IN PEOPLE WITH EMOTIONAL DISTURBANCE

Substance abuse is a common problem among people with emotional disturbance. Many people turn to drugs like marijuana, alcohol, and others to take away the pain they feel. However, drug abuse cannot truly relieve an emotional disturbance. It may mask the pain for a little while, but each time the individual sobers, he will find his emotional disturbance and the circumstances that caused it are still present. Worse yet, he will find his emotional disturbance compounded and in the long run made worse by his abuse of drugs.

Schools and communities have many programs such as D.A.R.E, M.A.D.D., S.A.D.D., Boys & Girls Clubs, and others to try to keep youth from taking drugs or drinking alcohol. Programs such as these recognize that the best treat-

Substance abuse often goes hand-in-hand with an emotional disturbance.

Alcohol and other drugs may mask emotional pain for a time, but ultimately, they cause more problems.

ment for substance abuse is prevention. For a person with emotional disturbance, the best way to prevent substance abuse is to find the source of her emotional disturbance and treat it. With the emotional relief proper treatment brings, she will not need drugs to help her overcome her pain and sorrow.

SUICIDE

Despite many people's best efforts to identify and help youth with emotional disturbance, the fact is that some young people go undiagnosed, and sometimes suicides occur.

    Boys with emotional disturbance are more likely to be overlooked for school services and counseling than girls are.

Many people speculate that this is because boys are expected to be aggressive and act out. Therefore, when a boy is showing signs of an emotional disturbance, his symptoms may be overlooked as a type of "boys will be boys" behavior. Girls, on the other hand, are not expected to act out in disruptive or violent ways, so when they do, they may be more likely to be identified as emotionally disturbed and receive the resources that will help them.

Not only are boys less likely to receive help for their emotional disturbance, they are also more likely to commit suicide. In fact, recent studies show that four times as many young men die of suicide than young women. However, the same studies show that three to four times more women attempt suicide than men.

How can three to four times more women than men attempt suicide, yet four times more men die of suicide than women? Researchers believe this strange statistic is due to the different ways in which men and women both communicate their emotional needs and attempt suicide. These studies have shown that when women attempt suicide, they are likely to use methods such as taking a large number of pills or slitting their wrists. Though these types of suicide attempts can do great and long-lasting harm and may result in death, such methods often fail to actually kill a person. Researchers believe that many of the women who choose these less-fatal methods do so because they don't really want to die. What they really want is for someone to help them, and there is nothing more powerful (or dangerous) than a suicide attempt to get someone to realize that something is truly wrong.

In contrast to the suicide methods that women choose, men tend to choose methods that are far more fatal, such as shooting themselves. Researchers **hypothesize** that most men communicate their needs differently than women do, often disguising their emotions and refusing to seek help.

More men than women hang themselves.

Researchers believe that in many cases, once a man has decided to commit suicide he has already passed the phase of seeking help. He has made up his mind that he actually wants to die and thus chooses a suicide method that has little chance of failure.

In the weeks before Trent commits suicide, Sheila notices that his life seems to be getting better. They have fun and relaxing conversations, laugh with one another, and forget their anger. Similarly, loved ones of people who have committed suicide often say that everything in the person's life suddenly seemed to be getting better during the final days of their loved one's life. They noticed that he was happier and more relaxed, that things seemed to be falling into place, that their loved one was finally getting order in his

A person who is preparing to commit suicide may seem more calm and relaxed in his final days.

life. He was completing tasks that had needed completing for a long time or visiting with people whom he had neglected.

Mental-health professionals warn families of people at risk for suicide to watch for this sign of people's lives seeming to get better directly before they commit suicide. The reason is that often, when a person has decided once and for all that he is going to commit suicide, that person will suddenly feel a great sense of relief. Knowing that on a certain date at a certain time all his troubles are going to end allows the individual to complete tasks, visit with people, and relax in a way he couldn't before. What many families interpret as their loved one finally starting to get better and gain control is actually their loved one taking care of final business before his death.

A wounded mind . . . can not cope with a broken world.
Escape seems the only option—but what we flee toward
will make all the difference.
—Theodora Carroll

7

RUNAWAY TRAIN

Sheila had become unhinged. The world spun around her like an amusement park ride out of control. She had hovered on the brink of disaster for so long, and now that disaster had come. Not wanting to end up like Trent, she had stopped cutting. But now she had no release for her emotions, and with Trent's death, her pain was worse than it had ever been before. In the daytime she lay on her bed, refusing to move. At night her rages ripped through the house like tornadoes, leaving an aftermath of smashed plates and overturned tables behind. Her father was so concerned he sent Megan to stay with an aunt for the week so that she wouldn't get injured in the path of one of Sheila's storms, but he had no idea what to do for Sheila.

On top of everything, a new danger was brimming. Sheila was refusing to eat. She found now that she couldn't cut, now that the world was spinning disaster around her, not eating was a new way to maintain control. She controlled her hunger in a way that she could not control her pain, and she deliberately starved herself until the hunger gnawed like a wild animal within her. Then she lay down and felt the hunger, felt it overwhelming her, felt it eating her alive, and the one comfort was that as long as she focused on the hunger in her body she could forget the hunger in her soul. Then when she did eat, she did so in tiny morsels, deliberately torturing herself by whetting her appetite, never eating enough to make the hunger go away. Like cutting, hunger was a distraction that had the power to mask the other pain, to make it fade just long enough that Sheila could tell herself it had died.

Unlike cutting, however, Sheila made no attempt to hide her new self-affliction. She was far beyond hiding now. Weak with hunger, burdened by pain, she did not have the energy to pretend. She didn't care who saw. She was stronger than all of them. They had hurt her, but she had formed an indomitable will that they were not going break. Her father said he wanted to take away her anger and pain—but look what happened to Trent when they took away his anger! Trent was right. Anger was strength. Anger was protection. When they came to take her away, to try to fix her, to make her normal, there would be no chinks in her armor.

But Sheila was not prepared for when her father invited Mara to the apartment.

Sheila had never let Mara come to her home before. If Mara saw Sheila's apartment, Sheila's room with the paint on the door and the conspicuous lack of lamps and other tabletop objects, she would figure out the truth. She'd know that Sheila wasn't who she claimed to be, that she was an imposter filled with anger and pain.

How could her father do this to her? Sheila wondered. How could he bring the one person she loved and respected to see her this way?

The three of them were seated in the tiny living room, Mara and Sheila's father holding juice glasses, a plate of food set temptingly on the table, but everyone knew this would not be a happy, social gathering.

Her father spoke first. "Sheila, Mara asked me if she could come." He ran his hands through his hair and shuffled his feet. Sheila hated him more than ever. "I just don't know what to do for you. Tell me what I can do to make you feel better." He wrung his hands as if he were attempting to squeeze water from the air. Sheila remained silent.

"Sheila," Mara spoke next. "I know you're in pain, but you have to let us help you." Sheila tried to control her anger as Mara spoke. She had never revealed her other side to Mara before, but now the war troops were marching up the steps within her, climbing to the surface like an invading army. Sheila struggled and fought, but she knew that soon there would be no keeping them down.

"Stop, Mara," she whispered, her words barely audible. "Please, Mara, stop."

"I can't stop, Sheila," Mara replied. "I'm afraid for you. You're not eating. You're not going to school. You won't let anyone see you."

"We don't want anything to happen to you," Sheila's father added, and the tension quickened. Sheila's emotions were dancing madly on the brink. She had never controlled such anger for so long, but what would happen if she kept holding it in? Would she explode like a supernova, incinerating everything within miles? Would she implode like a black hole, caving in upon herself and pulling everyone else in with her? Would the anger devour her until there was nothing left?

"We don't want what happened to Trent to happen to you."

The room fell silent. Mara had said it. Sheila hadn't thought Mara would have the guts, but she did. Suddenly, Sheila was gasping for breath. Something was on her chest, crushing her, suffocating her; she had to get it off.

Mara was still talking, as though she didn't notice that Sheila was fighting just to breathe. "Sheila, you have to get some help. You have to talk to someone, anyone. You have to go back to school. You have to eat."

Suddenly, the war was over. The invading army had won. Sheila was on her feet, screaming in Mara's face.

"Do you know why I don't eat, Mara?" Sheila wrenched her skirt away from her legs, revealing their hundreds of hairline scars, some only recently scabbed over, others the delicate pink of newly healed flesh, still others fading to white. The silence and shock in the room did nothing to deter Sheila from her rage. "Because if I don't starve myself, I'll have to cut myself instead!" she screamed, lifting her sleeve to reveal a striped arm. "And do you know what I'll do if I don't cut myself?" The veins stood out on Sheila's neck as her voice cracked at its highest possible pitch. Mara was shrinking before her. "I'll do this!" Sheila turned, grabbed the family's television, and yanked it to the floor. The screen imploded with a crash. "Can't you see? I'm out of control!" She rushed blindly, shoeless and directionless, out of the apartment.

Sheila arrived at Trent's house and threw herself against the door. For the first time in her memory, the door was locked. She stood for a moment, having no idea what to do. It did not even occur to her to knock. Instead she ran to the nearest window, took a rock, smashed the glass, and heedless of the sharp splinters that bit her legs and cut into her feet, climbed inside.

Inside, the house smelled the same, harbored the same darkness, but felt even emptier than it had before. No television flickered in the living room. No zombies reclined in the chairs. Sheila stood for a moment, spellbound by the quiet, feeling her racing heart beginning to calm and all the anger rolling into fear. She approached the basement door cautiously, not wanting to go through, afraid of what she might find, but knowing she had to see for herself.

When she opened the door, a puff of cool air rushed up, surrounded her, and lured her down into the dark. At first she held her breath (*would it smell?*) but then allowed a few tentative, shallow puffs of air. It smelled the same, damp and strangely clean. The bare bulbs cast the same eerie light. The dragon floated with wings spread and fiery breath streaming like always.

But the scene in the middle of the room pushed a gasp from Sheila's throat. The intricate diorama was obliterated, smashed to unrecognizable bits, and strewn like lifeless confetti all over the basement floor. Sheila fell to her knees, grasping at the bits and pieces of Trent's life's work, now nothing more than sand in her hands. "Why, why, why, why?" she whispered to herself over and over as the long repressed tears streamed down her face. She tilted her head back in anguish. There, stuck into the wall was Trent's pocketknife, and beside it carved in Trent's scrawling handwriting was her answer.

There was just too much hurt to cut out.

EMOTIONAL DISTURBANCE
AND EATING DISORDERS

Like self-injury and substance abuse, eating disorders are also common among people suffering from emotional disturbance. The two most common eating disorders are anorexia nervosa, in which an individual stops eating, and bulimia, in which an individual eats in large amounts and then vomits the food back up again.

After Trent's death, Sheila no longer wishes to cut herself. But she does wish to have the same control and emotional distraction that cutting herself provided. She finds anorexia to be a similar distraction. By strictly regulating the amount of food she eats, she feels like she has some control in her out-of-control life. Additionally, by starving herself, she can produce physical pain that distracts her from her emotional turmoil.

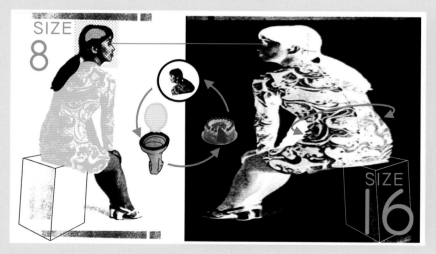

A person with an eating disorder may starve herself—or she may eat enormous quantities and then get rid of the food by vomiting.

A person with an emotional disturbance may long to feel as though he is in control of at least one area of his life.

The pattern that evolves in Sheila's behavior is typical of many people with undiagnosed or untreated emotional disturbance. Instead of addressing the sources of her emotional suffering, Sheila looks for distractions. She cuts herself to avoid succumbing to her anger. She uses drugs to make the anger temporarily go away. When she quits cutting, she starves herself. Her emotional disturbance appears to get better and worse over the course of her self-prescribed "treatments." While she cuts, she feels in control of her anger. When she is high, she feels free of her sorrow. While she starves herself, she feels in control of her emotional pain. However, the impression that her emotional disturbance diminishes in response to these behaviors is an illusion. All Sheila is really doing is replacing one unhealthy and dangerous behavior with another. She is never improving her emotional disturbance. Her emotional disturbance is simply being exhibited in different forms.

THE PAINFUL ISSUES OF ADOLESCENCE

Adolescence is a time of questions, exploration, and growth for young people. It is a time that carries much excitement, but also carries painful lessons and difficult emotional struggles. Painful parts of adolescence can be even more difficult for a person with an emotional disturbance.

Emotional Disturbance and the Family

Family dynamics, such as a parent leaving or a mother or father having inadequate parenting skills, are one of the risks factors for developing an emotional disturbance. To make matters more complicated, once the emotional disturbance exists, it further tears apart the already stressed family.

Many people try to treat emotional disturbance in young people through individual therapy that focuses specifically on the young person experiencing the disturbance. However, emotional disturbance often develops as a result of (among other factors) dynamics within the family and then goes on to affect the whole family. In most cases, family counseling in addition to individual counseling is more helpful than individual counseling alone. Family counseling, however, can be expensive and difficult for some families to attain. When a young person fits the criteria for an emotional disturbance, her school is required by law to provide her with appropriate support. However, although school officials meet with parents and attempt to involve parents in their child's education program, schools cannot provide in-depth support and counseling to an entire family. Many people with health insurance can receive counseling and support through their medical care. However, there are also

Family members may have difficulty understanding someone who has an emotional disturbance.

Relationships with peers are particularly important during adolescence.

many insurance companies that do not pay for this type of medical care. In addition, many people in the United States do not have any health insurance at all. In situations like these, families must look in other places for support. If there is an issue of abuse or neglect within the family, child and youth protective services will get involved. If there is not abuse or neglect within a family and therefore no access to social services, the family may go to churches, self-help groups, or other organizations in search of support.

Peer Relations

As discussed in chapter 2, peers play an incredibly important role in young people's lives. In general, young people place a great deal of emphasis on peer and friendship circles. Young people often worry about fitting in, having the right friends, and having peers think highly of them. Therefore, when youth are routinely rejected or bullied by their peers, they are at an increased risk of developing emotional disturbance. Furthermore, because young people often adjust their behavior to conform to that of their peers, youth whose friends are involved in reckless or criminal behavior or who have emotional disturbances themselves, are more likely to develop emotional disturbances as well.

On the other hand, as we see in Sheila's friendship with Mara, peers also play an incredibly positive role in young people's lives. When Trent and Sheila spent time together, they concentrated on their anger and pain, harmed themselves, and took drugs. When Mara and Sheila are together, however, they engage in healthy activities, have fun, and support each other. Her friendship with Mara makes Sheila want to stop cutting herself and become a happier, healthier person.

Sexuality

Exploring and questioning one's sexuality is a normal part of growing up—something that everyone experiences in some shape or form, and adolescence, puberty, and the teenage years are confusing for almost everyone. However, as young people become acutely sensitive to sexuality's new role in their lives, they sometimes target certain individuals who display differences in their sexuality for bullying at school. As we've already discussed, bullying at school places youth at increased risk for developing emotional disturbance, and bullying combined with emotional disturbance can make the inevitable process of exploring one's sexuality even more confusing and painful.

Sexuality plays a large role during the teenage years.

History and prejudice can also make the exploration of sexuality painful for young people. Many people once believed that individuals who were homosexual or bisexual were **deviant**. At one time, the *Diagnostic and Statistical Manual of Mental Disorders* even classified these forms of sexuality as mental disorders, and therefore forms of emotional disturbance. Today, however, psychiatrists, medical professionals, and much of the population realize that these forms of sexuality are not mental illnesses. Being homosexual or bisexual is *not* a form of emotional disturbance. For a young person who already has emotional disturbance, however, the explorations, questions, peer pressure, and fears of rejection that come with blossoming sexuality can be especially confusing and difficult.

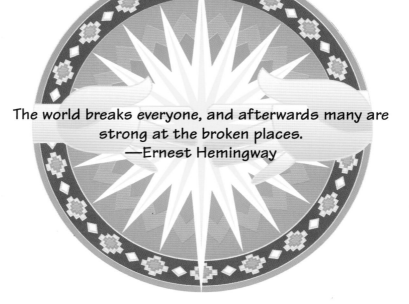

The world breaks everyone, and afterwards many are
strong at the broken places.
—Ernest Hemingway

8

WEATHERING THE STORM

Checking into the hospital's psychiatric unit was the most frightening thing Sheila had ever done. Her father and Mara stood, one on each side of her, like bookends to keep her standing. She grasped their hands, holding onto them for dear life, afraid she would sink, knowing she needed them if she was to get through this.

At the desk, she told the receptionist of her cutting; her starvation; her rages; her suicidal thoughts; how reality suddenly seemed warped, how they were all floating in an ocean, disconnected and unreal. Sheila had feared that some buzzer would ring, a red light would flash, "Crazy in the Hall!" would burst over the loudspeakers, and doctors in white coats would seize her and carry her away. But none of that happened. Everyone was smiling and calm. They checked her in, gave her a bed, and gave her some pills to fall asleep.

When she woke up, the sun was shining and two whole days had passed.

"I must have been tired," she said to the first nurse who entered the room.

"You sure were." He smiled. "And the medication probably helped a little bit, too."

When he left, Sheila dragged herself up to sitting and surveyed her surroundings. She had an *IV* for severe ***dehydration*** and a terrible hospital gown. The gown's short sleeves left Sheila no way to hide her scars, and for the first time she felt self-conscious about them. She hugged the thin blanket up to her neck.

A bouquet of flowers was on the side table. Sheila assumed it was from her father, but when she looked at the card it said, "Love, Meg." Looking at the card, Sheila realized she had been so wrapped up in her own troubles that she'd hardly spoken to her sister since . . . well . . . since their mother had left. Six years ago.

It suddenly dawned on Sheila. Six years of her life had gone by in pain and trauma. That was more than half of Megan's life. Sheila would have to get better so she could get to know her little sister.

She gazed out the window. The sun was warm and yellow, and flowers were blooming. When was the last time she'd enjoyed the sun or noticed a flower? Sheila didn't know. What she did know, however, was that this feeling of peace and well-being, newly awakened on a sunny world, would soon fade. There were difficult times ahead, perhaps harder than any she had weathered so far. But she still savored the morning calm and tried to make it last.

She must have drifted off to sleep again, because the next time she opened her eyes, her father was in the room.

"Awake!" He clapped, true happiness ringing in his voice. Sheila smiled at him and saw that her smile actually made him stand straighter, as though something heavy he'd been carrying on his shoulders had just lightened a little. "How are you feeling?"

"I'm feeling pretty good, Dad." She gave him another smile. "They have me on drugs. Can't you tell?" She laughed, but her father's face grew solemn. "Oh, it's a joke Dad. It's okay to laugh." Her father gave a smile, but it looked forced.

So they couldn't joke about her situation yet, that was okay. Sheila sighed. "I know it's going to get bad, but let's just enjoy this pleasant version of me for awhile, okay?"

"Yeah." Her dad gave a real smile this time. "Yeah, that's okay."

They sat quietly until the silence became uncomfortable.

Then Sheila's father told her about everything that had happened since she checked into the hospital. "I've taken some time off work." His voice contained a mixture of fear and pride. He had started working twelve-hour days when things first began going wrong with Sheila's mom, and he'd never let up since. "And Mara stayed here the whole first night, even though the nurses assured her you wouldn't be waking up for hours. She'll be coming again later today."

Megan had returned from her aunt's house and also wanted to visit. Sheila couldn't imagine why Megan would still subject herself to being in Sheila's presence, but she was glad for her little sister's determination.

After Sheila checked into the hospital, her father had notified her school as well.

"I can't go back to that school," Sheila replied matter-of-factly. "I need to go somewhere new, a place where I won't feel self-conscious and ridiculed all the time." As she made this request, Sheila felt fear licking in her stomach. It was the first fear she had felt since waking up, but she knew it would not be her last, and she tried to take a few calming breaths.

Her father looked pained. "A lot of people at that school care about you, Sheila. Mr. Hammond, your English teacher, art teacher, principal, the school psychologist, and I have all sat down together to talk about how we can make things better for you." Her father spoke quickly and nervously. Sheila could feel the fear turning to the same old anger. She took a breath, getting ready to fight, but her father held up his hand. "But none of that is going to happen right now." Sheila could tell her father was trying to soothe her. She concentrated on controlling the rising emotions while her father continued. "Right now everyone just wants you to get well. Later we can talk about school, but right now is time just for you, okay?" His eyes shone with a mixture of hope and desperation. Sheila tried to give in to his soothing and was surprised to find that she could control the emotions and keep them at bay.

Then Sheila's father told her about meeting the psychiatrist—

a seemingly smart woman, he said—who would come directly to their home to help all of them. Additionally, he had made an appointment to see a psychiatrist for himself as well. He seemed very proud of this step, and Sheila smiled to show that she was proud of him. Megan, too, would be speaking with a counselor.

"This has gone on long enough," Sheila's father said. "We're going to do something before it's too late. We're all going to do it together."

An hour passed, the first full hour Sheila could ever remember spending alone with her father. Then he left to pick up Megan from school. Minutes later, Mara came bustling in, her book bag on her shoulder. Sheila was afraid to look at Mara's face, so she inspected her IV and waited for Mara to speak.

"Great, you're up." Mara sounded chipper as always, and Sheila was encouraged to sneak a peak at her friend. When their eyes met, Mara smiled, but it didn't relieve Sheila's anxiety.

"Mara," she choked, afraid she wouldn't be able to get the words out, "I'm so sorry for everything. I never wanted you to know. . . ." She faltered. ". . . about the way I am."

Mara plopped onto the bed, sending Sheila bouncing. "Oh please, Sheila," Mara laughed. "I knew you were crazy from the first poem you ever read to me."

Sheila allowed herself to laugh as well, but she couldn't shake the nagging feeling that Mara would reject her.

"Look Sheila," Mara continued, serious this time, "we haven't been friends very long. But I feel like in this short time, I've come to know you better than I've ever known anyone." Mara stopped and thought for a moment. "You know, everyone's got problems, but most people are always trying to hide them and pretend that nothing's wrong. Everyone puts on a mask of being normal—but if we took off the normal masks, we'd find out that no one is normal at all. Everybody's faking."

Sheila thought about this for a moment. It seemed like a brilliant revelation. "So what you're saying," she ventured, a smile playing at her lips, "is that some people just have to fake it a little more than others."

"Exactly! And some people have to fake it a whole lot!"

Sheila joined in Mara's laughter. She hadn't laughed in a long time, and it felt good to laugh. But then Mara grew serious again. "You know, when you lost it at your apartment, that's the most real I have ever seen anyone be. No one has ever let me get that close to them before. It was frightening, but at the same time, it was like . . . there you were—your whole soul open for everyone to see. You're my best friend, Sheila, and I always want you to be your real self with me."

Sheila couldn't speak for a long time. No one had ever said anything so nice to her before. She didn't know how to thank Mara, but she knew she didn't have to. Finally, she ventured a joke. "Well, let's hope that psychiatrist can teach the real me not to throw things."

"Jeez, let's hope." Mara laughed. "Hey, I brought you something." She reached into her book bag and extracted the crumbling black journal that Sheila had been writing her thoughts and poetry in for years.

Sheila looked at it suspiciously. "Oh. . . ." Sheila was grateful for Mara's thoughtfulness, but she wasn't sure that she wanted to look at that book right now, maybe ever again. "You know, I don't think I want to go back to that book."

"Great!" Looking relieved, Mara dug further into her book bag. "'Cause I got you a new one!" She extracted a thick journal, bound in shiny purple cloth, and handed it to Sheila. On the front were two photographs. One was of Mara, the other of Sheila. They had been torn down the center and pasted together to make one picture. Mara had drawn funny arms onto the photograph to make the girls look like they were hugging. "We've never taken a photo of the two of us, so I had to paste two together." Now Mara was hesitant. "Do you think it's stupid?"

Sheila looked down at the funny journal. "No, Mara, it's wonderful."

That night, after visiting hours were over, Sheila cradled the new journal on her lap. It was the best gift she'd ever received. She was afraid to open it, afraid to write and mar it with her thoughts. But despite her fear, Sheila new what she had to do. After taking a deep breath and gathering her courage, she open the journal to its first clean, white page and started writing a new chapter to her life.

THE MULTISYSTEMIC APPROACH TO TREATMENT

In this final chapter, we see that Sheila is finally committing herself to trying to get well and overcome her emotional disturbance. In Sheila's case, however, getting well is not just about her receiving treatment. It's about her whole family reaching out for help and support. Sheila is not only going to see a psychiatrist to help her address deeply buried emotional issues, she's also going to change her educational and peer environment. She hopes to switch schools, not because the school does not have the resources to help her, but because she does not want to place herself back with the peers who bullied her. She has suffered through a serious

There are many steps that must be taken toward recovery—but there is hope for individuals with an emotional disturbance.

crisis and wishes to begin school in a new environment free of the risk factors her old school has. However, once she emerges from her current crisis, she may find that her teachers and psychologist are able to address the bullying problems and find a solution that won't require moving to a new school.

In addition to Sheila's personal steps toward recovery, her father will also be taking steps to aid in his daughter's recovery by focusing on bettering himself as a parent. He is going to see a psychiatrist to address his own emotional issues. Once he does so, he will be better equipped to address his daughter's emotional needs. He is going to take time off work so that he can focus completely on his family. He would also benefit from taking a parenting class and perhaps joining a support group for people who are divorced or for parents of children with emotional disturbance.

Sometimes family members or professionals may overlook the emotional needs of siblings of youth with emotional disturbance. Families and professionals may be so focused on addressing the needs of the child with emotional disturbance that they neglect to give the other child the attention she needs and deserves. Family counseling and individual counseling can help in addressing the needs of all family members.

Friends also play an important part in one's recovery. Everyone needs people whom they feel they can trust. Friends contribute to our sense of emotional well-being.

The multilayered approach to therapy is called a multisystemic approach. It focuses on multiple areas of treatment. Although emotional disturbance and other special needs are often addressed exclusively in the school setting, this type of therapy is a home-based form of care and usually has a different starting point than exclusively school-based care. For example, as in Sheila's case, an individual may be admitted to a hospital because she suffered a crisis and needed to be

Some young people find that music provides them with an emotional outlet.

in an environment where professionals could be sure she was safe from self-harm. When she leaves the hospital, however, she will return home and her therapist will visit her home, school, and other community settings to determine what risk factors she faces, where those risk factors are, and how best to address them.

As you learned earlier, children with emotional disturbance often have multiple risk factors and circumstances contributing to their emotional condition. Laws like IDEA guarantee that a child's special needs be met in the educational setting, but they do not guarantee that services be extended to the child outside of school. To be truly successful, therapy must address all the risk factors and circumstances influencing the child. Since the family is the major environ-

A child with an emotional disturbance needs treatment at multiple levels.

No child should be thrown away. Each individual is worth saving.

mental influence on a child, the family often needs just as much attention as the child with emotional disturbance needs. Emotional disturbance does not simply happen without reason. It is the affect of certain causes. Those causes must be addressed if one wishes to have the best outcome from therapy. Many types of therapies concentrate only on treating the child. However, the child must then return to the environment and risk factors contributing to his emotional disturbance. In multisystemic therapy, the child's entire community is engaged in the treatment process. Parents may attend therapy sessions and parenting classes; neighbors may be asked to help watch children; other family members (like grandparents, aunts, and uncles) may be asked to join in the therapy process. The school will be contacted and intricately involved. Social workers are often part of a treatment team for the child and family, and the child and the family are treated as one interconnected unit. Improvements for one aspect of the unit mean improvements for the whole.

FURTHER READING

Adamec, Christine. *How to Live With a Mentally Ill Person: A Handbook of Day-to-Day Strategies.* New York: John Wiley and Sons, 1996.

Alderman, Tracy. *The Scarred Soul: Understanding and Ending Self-inflicted Violence.* Oakland, Calif.: New Harbinger Publications, 1997.

Kaysen, Susanne. *Girl, Interrupted* (Reprint Edition). New York: Vintage Books, 1994.

Kettlewell, Caroline. *Skin Game.* New York: Griffin Trade Paperback, 2000.

Kindlon, Daniel J. *Raising Cain: Protecting the Emotional Life of Boys.* New York: Ballantine Books, 2000.

Pipher, Mary. *Reviving Ophelia: Saving the Selves of Adolescent Girls.* New York: Ballantine Books, 2002.

Psychiatric Disorders: Drugs and Psychology for the Mind and Body (15-book series). Philadelphia: Mason Crest Publishers, 2003.

Sacker, Ira M. and Marc A. Zimmer. *Dying to be Thin: Understanding and Defeating Anorexia Nervosa and Bulimia—A Practical, Lifesaving Guide* (Updated Edition). New York: Warner Books, 2001.

Strong, Marilee. *A Bright Red Scream: Self-mutilation and the Language of Pain.* New York: Penguin Books, 1998.

Woolis, Rebecca and Agnes Hatfield. *When Someone You Love Has a Mental Illness: A Handbook for Families, Friends, and Caregivers.* Los Angeles: J.P. Tarcher, 1992.

Wurtzel, Elizabeth. *Prozac Nation: Young and Depressed in America: A Memoir.* New York: Riverhead Books, 1997.

FOR MORE INFORMATION

American Academy of Child and Adolescent Psychiatry
www.aacap.org

Federation of Families for Children's Mental Health
www.ffcmh.org

The InterNetwork for Youth
www.in4y.com

KidSource Online (Education and health-care information for parents
   and children)
www.kidsource.com

National Alliance for the Mentally Ill
www.nami.org

National Clearinghouse on Families and Youth
www.ncfy.com

National Information Center for Children and Youth with Disabilities
www.nichcy.org

National Mental Health Association
www.nmha.org

National Runaway Switchboard
www.nrscrisisline.org

S.A.F.E. Alternatives (Self-Abuse Finally Ends)
www.selfinjury.com

The Sidran Institute (Information about trauma-related stress disorders)
www.sidran.org

Publisher's Note:

The Web sites listed in this section were active at the time of publication. The publisher is not responsible for Web sites that have changed their address or discontinued operation since the date of publication. The publisher will review and update the Web sites upon each reprint.

GLOSSARY

absolve: To relieve of guilt, blame, obligation, or responsibility.

adept: Skilled.

angst: A feeling of anxiety or insecurity.

chronic: Lasting for a long time or recurring.

cognitive therapy: Psychiatric therapy that focuses on exploring (usually through talking) a person's mental processes such as thought, reasoning, judgment and behavior, and then working to change those processes.

conformists: People who adjust their activities, manner, dress, behavior, etc., to be like that of the majority of other people.

cynical: Suspicious and scornful of other people's motives and virtue.

dehydration: The condition where body fluids are depleted.

delusions: False beliefs held despite all evidence to the contrary.

developmental: Of or related to one's development.

deviant: Differing from the norm.

diagnostic criteria: The requirements necessary to meet a medical diagnosis.

environmental: Of or relating to the environment or surrounding conditions.

exhibitions: Displays or performances.

facade: A false appearance.

fatigue: A feeling of weariness or exhaustion.

grunge: A form of "alternative music," featuring heavy guitar, drumming, and vocals. It was made popular in the 1980s and 1990s by Seattle-based bands like Nirvana, Stone-Temple Pilots, Pearl Jam, and others. Grunge bands and music formed as a rebellion to the "pop" music mass-produced by big record companies.

homicidal: Desiring or seeking to kill another person.

hypothesize: To make a tentative assumption.

impoverished: Experiencing poverty. Lacking money or resources.

indicative: Indicating. A sign or clue of something else.

integral: Centrally important.

IV: An intravenous line; used to administer fluids or nutrition directly into the blood vessels.

manic: Affected by mania—violent behavior, a craze, or excessive enthusiasm and desire.

obsessive-compulsive disorder: A psychiatric disorder characterized by anxiety, fixation on unwanted feelings and thoughts, the performance of personal rituals—repetitive hand washing for example—and the inability to control these feelings, thoughts, and actions.

peer: A person of one's same age, rank, or status.

poetry slam: An event in which poets gather to read their work, often using props like instruments, costumes, etc., and get judged, usually by the audience members, creating a competition between the poets. The best advance and compete against each other until a winner is determined.

provocation: Something that encourages or drives a person to perform an action.

psychotic: Having a distorted sense of reality often accompanied by acute anxiety and paranoia.

rationalize: To find reasons or excuses for one's behavior or thinking.

schizophrenia: A psychiatric disorder characterized by psychotic behavior in which a person is unable to tell the difference between reality and delusion, has illogical thoughts, and suffers from hallucinations.

self-esteem: One's feeling toward and estimation of oneself.

Sodom and Gomorrah: Ancient cities in Palestine that according to the Judeo-Christian Bible were destroyed by God because of sinfulness.

spectrum: An array or distribution of characteristics.

stigma: A mark of disgrace.

suicidal: Desiring or seeking to kill oneself.

temperament: A person's manner, behavior, or typical way of being.

trepidation: A sense of fear or apprehension.

INDEX

BIOGRAPHIES

Autumn Libal is a graduate of Smith College and works as a freelance writer and illustrator in Northeastern Pennsylvania. She has written for other Mason Crest series, including NORTH AMERICAN FOLKLORE, NORTH AMERICAN INDIANS TODAY, and PSYCHIATRIC DISORDERS: DRUGS AND PSYCHOLOGY FOR THE MIND AND BODY.

Dr. Lisa Albers is a developmental behavioral pediatrician at Children's Hospital Boston and Harvard Medical School, where her responsibilities include outpatient pediatric teaching and patient care in the Developmental Medicine Center. She currently is Director of the Adoption Program, Director of Fellowships in Developmental and Behavioral Pediatrics, and collaborates in a consultation program for community health centers. She is also the school consultant for the Walker School, a residential school for children in the state foster care system.

Dr. Carolyn Bridgemohan is an instructor in pediatrics at Harvard Medical School and is a board-certified developmental behavioral pediatrician on staff in the Developmental Medicine Center at Children's Hospital, Boston. Her clinical practice includes children and youth with autism, hearing impairment, developmental language disorders, global delays, mental retardation, and attention and learning disorders. Dr. Bridgemohan is coeditor of *Bright Futures Case Studies for Primary Care Clinicians: Child Development and Behavior*, a curriculum used nationwide in pediatric residency training programs.

Cindy Croft is the State Special Needs Director in Minnesota, coordinating Project EXCEPTIONAL MN, through Concordia University. Project EXCEPTIONAL MN is a state project that supports the inclusion of children in community settings through training, on-site consultation, and professional development. She also teaches as adjunct faculty for Concordia University, St. Paul, Minnesota. She has worked in the special needs arena for the past fifteen years.

Dr. Laurie Glader is a developmental pediatrician at Children's Hospital in Boston where she directs the Cerebral Palsy Program and is a staff pediatrician with the Coordinated Care Services, a program designed to meet the needs of children with special health care needs. Dr. Glader also teaches regularly at Harvard Medical School. Her work with public agencies includes New England SERVE, an organization that builds connections between state health departments, health care organizations, community providers, and families. She is also the staff physician at the Cotting School, a school specializing in the education of children with a wide range of special health care needs.